BELLES

A play in two acts
and
Thirty-nine phone calls

By Mark Dunn

Samuel French, Inc.

✗✗✗✗✗✗✗✗✗✗✗✗✗✗✗✗✗✗✗✗✗✗✗✗✗✗✗✗✗

BURIED TREASURE FROM SAMUEL
FRENCH, INC.

Most of the superb plays listed below have never been produced in New York City. Does this mean they aren't "good enough" for New York? JUDGE FOR YOURSELF!

ABOUT FACE -- AN ACT OF THE IMAGINATION -- ALL SHE CARES ABOUT IS THE YANKEES -- ALONE AT THE BEACH -- AMERICAN CANTATA -- THE ANASTASIA FILE -- ARCHANGELS DON'T PLAY PINBALL -- THE BAR OFF MELROSE -- BEDROOMS -- BEYOND REASONABLE DOUBT -- BILL W. AND DR. BOB -- BINGO -- BLUE COLLAR BLUES -- BODYWORK -- BRONTE -- CARELESS LOVE -- CAT'S PAW -- CHEKHOV IN YALTA -- A CHORUS OF DISAPPROVAL -- CINCINNATI -- THE CURATE SHAKESPEARE AS YOU LIKE IT -- DADDY'S DYIN' -- DANCERS -- DARKSIDE -- ELIZABETH -- FIGHTING CHANCE -- FOOLIN' AROUND WITH INFINITY -- GETTING THE GOLD -- GILLETTE -- THE GIRLHOOD OF SHAKESPEARE'S HEROINES -- GOD'S COUNTRY --- IMAGINARY LINES -- INTERPRETERS -- LLOYD'S PRAYER -- MAKE IN BANGKOK -- MORE FUN THAN BOWLING -- OWNERS -- PAPERS -- PIZZA MAN -- POSTMORTEM -- PRAVDA -- THE PUPPETMASTER OF LODZ - THE REAL QUEEN OF HEARTS AIN'T EVEN PRETTY -- RED NOSES -- RETROFIT -- RETURN ENGAGEMENTS -- THE RIVERS AND RAVINES -- ROBIN HOOD -- SHIVAREE -- A SMALL FAMILY BUSINESS -- STAINED GLASS -- TAKE A PICTURE -- TALES FROM HOLLYWOOD -- TEN NOVEMBER -- THEATER TRIP -- THIS ONE THING I DO -- THIS SAVAGE PARADE -- TRAPS -- THE VOICE OF THE PRAIRIE -- WIDOW'S WEEDS -- THE WISTERIA BUSH -- THE WOMAN IN BLACK

Consult our most recent Catalogue for details.

✗✗✗✗✗✗✗✗✗✗✗✗✗✗✗✗✗✗✗✗✗✗✗✗✗✗✗✗✗

BELLES

A play in two acts
and
Thirty-nine phone calls

By Mark Dunn

SAMUEL FRENCH, INC.
45 WEST 25TH STREET   NEW YORK 10010
7623 SUNSET BOULEVARD   HOLLYWOOD 90046
LONDON   *TORONTO*

Copyright © 1989 by Mark Dunn

ISBN 0 573 69141 X   Printed in U.S.A.

74566280

for Mary

IMPORTANT BILLING AND CREDIT REQUIREMENTS

Those who always speak well of women
do not know them enough:
Those who always speak ill of them
do not know them at all.

Pigualt-Lebrun

BELLES was first presented at Texas Woman's University in Denton, Texas on January 29, 1988. It was directed by Mary Lou Hoyle. The scenery was designed by Mary E. Murdock. The lighting was by Charles E. Harrill. The costumes were designed by Jamelle Flowers. The production stage manager was Thom Talbott. The cast, in order of appearance, was as follows:

PEGGY	Terri Zagrodnick
ANEECE	Shanon Clark-Boaze
ROSEANNE	Lori Latiolais
AUDREY	Denise Joann Yeatts
DUST	Janet A. Mikealson
PAIGE	Shelly Sanders

BELLES opened in New York City on April 5, 1989 at the Thirteenth Street Repertory Company. It was directed by Seth Gordon. The set was by Ann Davis. The lighting was designed by Tim Noble. The costumes were by Patrick Lucey. The sound was by Peter J. Daly. Original music was written by Andy Bloor. The production stage manager was Wendy Ouellette. The cast, in order of appearance, was as follows:

PEGGY	Judith Pucci
ANEECE	Linda Mason Pease
ROSEANNE	Jean Sorich
AUDREY	Valerie Gilbert
DUST	Dyan Kane
PAIGE	June Schreiber

Special music written for the Thirteenth Street Repertory Company production of *BELLES* is available from the composer. Please contact:

Andrew Bloor
160 W. 71st Street
Suite 19F
New York, NY 10023

The Belles

Peggy Reece, age 40, Memphis, Tennessee, (Area Code 901)

Aneece Walker, age 37, Philadelphia Pennsylvania (Area Code 215)

Roseanne Johnson, age 29, Atlanta, Georgia (Area Code 404)

Audrey Hart, age 32, Collierstown, Mississippi (Area Code 601)

Sherry "Dust" Walker, age 30, Elk Run, Washington (Area Code 206)

Paige Walker, age 19, Austin, Texas (Area Code 512)

Where the Bells Ring

The stage is divided into six distinct sections or "mini-sets," all visible to the audience as the play begins. The stage should not have a cluttered, crowded look: each area should be furnished with as little furniture and as few props as possible to suggest the following:

> Peggy Reese's sitting room
> Aneece Walker's bedroom
> Roseanne Johnson's kitchen
> Audrey Hart's den
> Sherry "Dust" Walker's "living space"
> Paige Walker's dormitory room

Each of the six areas of the stage will also require its own lighting; the play will sometimes resemble a split-screen montage, with our attention moving quickly from one telephone to another as conversations start and finish or alternate between two or more of the sisters.

When the Bells Ring

From a Friday evening to the following Monday during early fall of this year.

ACT I

*AT RISE: LIGHTS come up on: the six telephones.
One by one they begin to RING until all are
SINGING OUT in a CACOPHONY of
DINGLING and JINGLING – then abrupt
silence and DARKNESS.*

*After a moment, LIGHTS come up on the
telephone alcove of Peggy Reese and her
mother's sitting room. It is FRIDAY NIGHT.
PEGGY enters carrying a pad and pencil.
SHE sits down at a small writing table and
pulls the telephone to her. SHE makes a check
mark on the pad, then dials a number.
LIGHTS come up in Aneece Walker's empty
bedroom as the phone on her nightstand
RINGS. After three or four RINGS, ANEECE
rushes in from the bathroom. SHE is wrapped
in a towel and dripping wet.*

ANEECE. Hello?
PEGGY. Aneece?
ANEECE. Who is it?
PEGGY. It's Peggy.
ANEECE. I'm wet, Peggy.
PEGGY. This will only take a minute.
ANEECE. I'm drenching the carpet.

9

PEGGY. It's about Mama.
ANEECE. I'll call you back.

(*ANEECE hangs up and returns to the bathroom. PEGGY glances at her wristwatch.*)

PEGGY. A record ten seconds, Aneece. Our longest telephone conversation yet.

(*SHE hangs up and dials another number. LIGHTS come up in Roseanne Johnson's kitchen. ROSEANNE is tinkering with a blender. The phone RINGS.*)

ROSEANNE. (*Answering.*) William?
PEGGY. No. It's Peggy.
ROSEANNE. (*Surprised.*) *Peggy?* Are you here in Atlanta?
PEGGY. No. I'm at home.
ROSEANNE. You sound so clear. You sound like you're right next door. I want Melissa and Melanie to hear this connection. (*Calling.*) Melissa!
PEGGY. Wait, Roseanne. You don't need to —
ROSEANNE. You're the sweetest one to call. How's Mama?
PEGGY. That's what I phoned about.
ROSEANNE. (*Alarmed.*) Is it her heart?
PEGGY. No. She ate some bad tuna.
ROSEANNE. Tuna? Tuna fish?

PEGGY. Yes, Rose. I had to take her to Methodist Central.

ROSEANNE. Lord, Peggy. That woman's the daughter of Job. You just know if there's bad tuna out there, Mama'll make a sandwich out of it.

(*During the following exchange between Peggy and Roseanne, ANEECE – wearing a robe – returns to her bedroom. SHE picks up the telephone. Not remembering the number, SHE stops to look it up, then dials.*)

PEGGY. The doctor said she'll be fine.

ROSEANNE. (*Thinking aloud.*) How do they know it was the tuna and not the mayonnaise?

PEGGY. (*Impatiently.*) It wasn't a sandwich, Rose. It was a tuna and tomato star.

ROSEANNE. A what?

PEGGY. A tuna and tomato star. There was no mayonnaise.

ROSEANNE. Then what holds it all together?

(*ANEECE, obviously hearing a busy signal, hangs up.*)

ANEECE. (*Reassuringly to herself.*) It's hemorrhoids again. Peggy wants to share Mama's hemorrhoids with all of us.

(*SHE goes back into the bathroom as ROSEANNE sees something out her kitchen window.*)

ROSEANNE. (*Shouting out the window without covering the phone mouthpiece.*) MELISSA ANN JOHNSON, IF YOU DON'T GIVE YOUR SISTER SOME OF THAT SNO-CONE I'M GOING TO WRING YOUR NECK. SANTA'S WATCHING YOU, YOUNG LADY. (*Back into phone.*) Did they pump her stomach?

PEGGY. (*Recuperating from damaged ear drums.*) She didn't say.

ROSEANNE. You should have called me sooner. I should have been there with her.

PEGGY. She was only in the hospital for a day and a half.

ROSEANNE. (*Her attention again drawn outside; shouting:*) LEAVE IT. JUST LEAVE IT. NO, YOU MAY NOT PICK THE DIRT OFF.

PEGGY. I'll let you go.

ROSEANNE. (*Ignoring this.*) I can't find anything in this kitchen, Peggy. This morning Melissa had to carry her lunch to school in a worn-out Rich's shopping bag. She died of embarrassment. There are gremlins in this kitchen, Peggy. They break my blender and hide my girls' lunch boxes.

PEGGY. I need to go, Rose. We'll talk later.

ROSEANNE. You give Mama my love.

PEGGY. I will.

(*Both PEGGY and ROSEANNE hang up. ROSEANNE looks out the window, shakes her*

*head disconsolately and returns to the blender
as LIGHTS fade out in her kitchen. LIGHTS
come up in Audrey Hart's den. The telephone
sits on a small table next to an old, overstuffed
armchair. Across from the chair are a trophy
cabinet which houses several hunting
trophies, and a tiny child's chair facing
upstage. PEGGY dials again. Audrey's phone
RINGS. AUDREY enters wearing a black
strapless gown with a bright red heart
appliqued on her chest.)*

AUDREY. (*Answering.*) Audrey — thump,
thump — Hart.

PEGGY. Audrey, it's Peggy.

AUDREY. (*Excitedly.*) Oh, Peg, you're not
going to believe what has happened. I got myself a
bona fide engagement.

PEGGY. That's wonderful.

AUDREY. Now the club we're booked in — it's
clear over to Vicksburg, but I really don't mind.
Me and Rothschild, we'd take our act all the way
down to New Orleans for a chance like this.

PEGGY. I'd like to hear more about it, Audrey,
but I have some family business.

AUDREY. It's Mama, isn't it?

PEGGY. Yes.

AUDREY. I knew it. Her heart stopped again.
Was she at home or at the mall?

PEGGY. It wasn't her heart. She ate some bad
tuna.

AUDREY. You mean she was *poisoned?*

PEGGY. It had some bacteria or something in it. I took her to the hospital.

AUDREY. Poor Mama.

PEGGY. She's better now.

AUDREY. They pumped her stomach?

PEGGY. I don't know.

AUDREY. Probably the bravest woman I've ever met. Can I do anything?

PEGGY. Thank you, but she's all right now.

AUDREY. You know what? If I tell Harry about it, he'll have me tossing out every box of Tuna Helper in the house. (*A sudden thought.*) Hang on. Someone wants to talk to you. (*Drops the phone and goes to the child's chair.*)

PEGGY. (*Apparently realizing what Audrey is about to do.*) Wait, Audrey — I don't really have time. Audrey?

(*AUDREY picks up the occupant of the chair: a ventriloquist's dummy dressed in a suit. SHE returns to the phone and places the receiver to the dummy's ear, the speaker to its mouth.*)

AUDREY. (*As her dummy, Rothschild.*) Hello 'dere, 'eggy. How ya doin'?

PEGGY. I can't hear you, Audrey. I can't hear what you're saying.

AUDREY. (*Continuing as Rothschild, overlapping Peggy.*) It's me — Rothschild! I'm an investment counselor, now. Yuk, yuk, yuk.

PEGGY. Pick up the phone, Audrey.

AUDREY. (*Still as Rothschild.*) I get rich reading Standard and Poors. Get it? Yuk, yuk, yuk.

PEGGY. For God's sake, Audrey, pick up the phone.

AUDREY. (*Still as Rothschild.*) Don't get much sleep though. That's why I got money bags under my eyes. Yuk, yuk.

(*PEGGY hangs up the phone. AUDREY takes her phone handset from the dummy.*)

AUDREY. Still cute as a button, huh? Peggy? Hello?

(*LIGHTS fade out in Audrey's den. LIGHTS come up in Paige Walker's empty dorm room. PEGGY dials. The phone RINGS several times. PEGGY counts off the rings to herself. No one enters to answer and SHE hangs up. Paige's dorm room returns to DARKNESS. PEGGY dials another number. LIGHTS come up in Dust Walker's "living space." DUST, dressed in leotards, is doing stretches on the floor. Her telephone, a speaker phone, RINGS on the floor beside her.*)

DUST. (*Answering with the punch of a button as SHE continues her stretches.*) I greet you.

PEGGY. Hello?

DUST. Greetings to you and yours.

PEGGY. Sherry?

DUST. No one here by *that* name.

PEGGY. (*Suspiciously.*) It sounds like you, Sherry.

DUST. Well, there once was a Sherry here. And yes, she *did* occupy this body for a time, but she is no longer within.

PEGGY. (*Reluctantly playing along.*) So who took her place?

DUST. The chaff which blows in the wind. You may call me "Dust."

PEGGY. *Dust?*

DUST. I am omnipresent. I am the marriage of earth and time.

PEGGY. Last month you were a colander.

DUST. Not *a* colander, Peggy dear. Just "Colander."

PEGGY. Look – Mama was in the hospital.

DUST. Was it her heart?

PEGGY. No, it was food poisoning. She ate some bad fish.

DUST. I'm glad you called me. Should I send a card?

PEGGY. I think Mama would like that.

DUST. That time her heart stopped at Krogers I didn't send a card. I felt miserable for days. I mean the woman *is* my mother.

PEGGY. She's much better now. I'll call again next week.

DUST. (*Not about to end the conversation so soon.*) I had this revelation last night, Peggy. It came to me in a dream.

PEGGY. Just how long was this dream?

DUST. I don't know. I'll capsulize it for you. There were three figures standing in the shadows beside my bed — St. Thomas Aquinas, Emily Dickinson, and Buddy Hackett.

(*The receiver still to her ear, PEGGY slowly and wearily brings her head to rest on the surface of the writing table.*)

DUST. No, come to think of it, Buddy was not standing. He was rolling around on the floor. I think Emily had just hit him in the head with her chapbook.

(*LIGHTS go out on PEGGY and DUST, and come up in Audrey's den. AUDREY sits in her armchair with Rothschild balanced on one knee, practicing her routine. SHE holds a glass of water in her free hand.*)

AUDREY. My, but it's a warm night tonight. Rothschild, tell the good folks what happened to you at work this morning.

(*SHE takes a big drink from the glass as SHE moves Rothschild's mouth. SHE says something completely unintelligible, water*)

dribbling out one side of her mouth. SHE
swallows, then turns to Rothschild.)

AUDREY. Needs a little work, doesn't it?

(SHE makes Rothschild nod. SHE sets the water
glass down, picks up the phone, and dials. Into
the phone:)

AUDREY. Patsy Bordon, please. (*She*
straightens Rothschild's tie as SHE waits for
Patsy to come to the phone.) Patsy? This is
Audrey. I was wondering — could you get off a
couple hours early tonight to come see me and
Rothschild? ... But I really need you there. For
moral support. I get the worst butterfl-- ... He's up
in the Ozarks with Amos. ... You know Harry —
hunting's in the man's blood. If he doesn't get out
once a month and bag himself something he can
show off at the Friendship Meat Locker, he
becomes like a caged animal. He starts pacing
back and forth and grumbling about how he can
hear the call of the wild and it knows his name.
... We really could use a friendly face in the
audience tonight, Patsy. Those club regulars can
be extremely tough on new talent. ... Well, if old
Simon Lagree has a change of heart, Rothschild
and me will be at Reba's Rendezvous Lounge on I-
20 just east of Vicksburg. I got a lot of new
material you've never heard. Stuff about the stock
market and mutual funds and — there's this one

part in the act where we get into this play-like argument when I tell Rothschild that all my money's tied up in a low-interest savings account. He calls me a weenie and I start to cry. ... Nor for *real,* silly, but that audience won't know the difference.

(*LIGHTS fade out on AUDREY and Rothschild and come up on DUST sitting cross-legged on the floor, phone to her ear.*)

DUST. Hello, Western Union? ... My name is Dust Walker. Yes, Dust. D-U-S-T Walker. I've never sent a telegram before. I prefer the telephone but I have a very delicate situation here concerning my loverman. I think my purposes would be better served by a good old-fashioned Western Union telegram ... Mailgram then. I had a dream about a telegram once. It was delivered by the little bellboy on TV — the one who always goes: (*SHE cups her hand around her mouth.*) "Call fora Pheelip Moerriss." (*Lowers her hand.*) Except in my dream he's going: (*She cups her hand again.*) "Telegra-yam fora Sherry Walker." (*Lowers her hand.*) That's back when I was Sherry. ... Yes, it's a short dream. Anyway, the boy — or was it a midget? Sometimes you can't tell the difference if they don't have facial hair. Doesn't matter. He hands me this telegram and I rip it open — I've never been sent a telegram before and I can't wait to see who it could be from so I rip it right open and start to read it and discover it's all in a language I can't understand. Or maybe it's not even in a foreign language at all because some of the words are all consonants — you can't even pronounce them. And here's the really weird part: It turns out that the telegram is from — well, it's from *me. Me!* And I look at the boy or the smooth-shaven midget — whoever — and I say, "Mr. Bellboy — I cannot read this. I cannot read this telegram at all." And he shakes his head and says, "But Ms. Walker, *you* are the one who sent it." Then he turns into a goat and eats the telegram right out of my hand. What do you think of *that?* ... Yes, I have everything I want to say right here.

(*SHE produces several scraps of paper. It should be immediately apparent that there is too much there to relay by means of a telegram.*)

DUST. Let me get the pages in order first. (*SHE sifts through the papers.*) Perhaps I should find out how much this is going to cost before we get started. ... (*incredulously.*) Does that include punctuation? ... (*A ploy to get off the phone.*) Oh my God! My house is on fire! (*SHE hangs up quickly and thinks for a moment.*) Well, it will just have to be the telephone. (*SHE picks up the handset, starts to dial, loses courage and hangs up. A deep breath, another attempt also abandoned at the last minute. SHE hangs up and finds a nice*

*spot to stand on her head. LIGHTS go out over
DUST as LIGHTS come up in Paige's dormitory
room just as SHE is entering.)*

PAIGE. *(To herself.)* Losers. Everyone of
them. Losers.

*(SHE flops down on the bed. Aneece's bedroom
LIGHTS come up. ANEECE enters from the
bathroom. SHE is dressed formally. SHE sits
down on the bed by her telephone. PAIGE picks
up her phone and dials. ANEECE picks up her
phone before it rings. ANEECE listens; SHE
looks puzzled. SHE depresses the plunger a
couple of times.)*

ANEECE. Damn!
PAIGE. What?
ANEECE. Hello?
PAIGE. Aneece?
ANEECE. Who *is* this?
PAIGE. It's Paige.
ANEECE. Paige? I thought the phone was
dead.
PAIGE. You didn't let it ring, stupid.
ANEECE. *(Sarcastically.)* I'm sorry. Call me
back. I'll let it ring and ring.
PAIGE. No. It was just freaky. That's all.
Like those times when you say the devil's on the
line.
ANEECE. What are you talking about?

PAIGE. You know, Aneece. Like when you're on the phone with somebody and you start hearing funny noises. Then one of you has to say, "Devil's on the line" and change phone ears as fast as you can or you're liable to go straight to hell.

ANEECE. (*Half-heartedly playing along.*) Is he on the line now?

PAIGE. God, I hope not. (*SHE thinks about this, then moves the receiver to the other ear.*) Listen, I need some big sisterly advice.

ANEECE. About what?

PAIGE. Guys.

ANEECE. Guys? That's hardly my department.

PAIGE. Sure it is. You work with a lot of men. You *know* men. So here's the thing — say you've been going out with two, maybe three different guys a week and they're starting to become like real turnoffs to you because they're only into the physical thing.

ANEECE. And you're not?

PAIGE. What?

ANEECE. Nothing. Go on.

PAIGE. Okay. You know you have to draw the line somewhere or else you're going to find yourself making it with harelips and guys with no color in their eyeballs. But they don't believe anything you say because they've all heard about your reputation. Anyway, it really *is* getting monotonous to me and I really do want to slow things down until the right one comes along.

ANEECE. (*Obligated to respond.*) Certainly.

PAIGE. You know, Aneece – these guys – they aren't even very subtle anymore. Like this last bozo who said to me right during the best part of that Stephen King movie where the people keep exploding – he said, "Paige, I want to cup your tumid breasts in my hands." I don't even know what "tumid" means!

ANEECE. The problem is – you haven't been very selective.

PAIGE. (*Disappointed.*) I know *that*, Aneece.

ANEECE. You need to exercise better judgment.

PAIGE. But I can't. That's the thing. I look at them for the first time and they all seem normal. Then after a while they turn into Dr. Jekyll.

ANEECE. Mr. Hyde. Did Peggy call you?

PAIGE. No. I mean I wouldn't know. I was out.

ANEECE. She wanted to tell me something about Mama.

PAIGE. You think something's wrong?

ANEECE. I don't know.

PAIGE. Did it sound urgent?

ANEECE. Yes. But then Peggy can make a hangnail sound urgent. Listen, Paige, you've caught me at a bad time. We'll talk later, okay?

PAIGE. Sure.

(*THEY both hang up – LIGHTS come up on PEGGY at her writing table. ALL THREE*

dial their phones at the same time. We hear a
chorus of BUSY SIGNALS. THEY hang up,
then simultaneously try again. Once more,
the BUSY SIGNALS. LIGHTS go out in all
three rooms. MUSIC plays. LIGHTS come up
on ROSEANNE in her kitchen. SHE is sitting
on the floor, the phone to her ear. The electric
blender is in many pieces now, spread out in
front of her. SHE has been crying.)

ROSEANNE. (*Into phone.*) Hello, Suicide
Prevention? ... Yes, I'll hold. (*SHE leans back*
against the storage door beneath the counter and
pulls her knees up to her chest.) Yes, I'm still
here. I got your number out of the phone book.
Really, I'm not suicidal but I do need someone to
talk to. I hope you don't mind me tying up this line
when there might be people with slit wrists trying
to get through. (*Answering a question.*) I'm on the
floor of my kitchen. The linoleum is very dingy.
I take full responsibility. (*Answering another*
question.) Well, there are some cleansers and
things under the sink but I assure you I wouldn't
ingest them. I have two young daughters. And a
husband. And I should mention my sisters. I have
five of them. I know you're probably wondering
with five sisters what's this woman calling *me*
for? You'd think I'd feel comfortable talking to at
least one of them but we all have so little in
common these days. Aneece and Paige and the
one whose name keeps changing — they've never

been married. Audrey's married but she's got this
little boy made of wood. ... Yes, wood. I can't
relate to that. And Peggy's been taking care of our
mother since Peg's husband Vincent died a couple
of years ago. ... Well, I get so sad sometimes. The
least little thing clouds up my whole day. You
know, from your voice I can't tell if you're a man
or a woman. Is that done mechanically on purpose
or do you just have an above average number of
hormones of the opposite sex? I read about that in
McCalls.

(*LIGHTS come up on PAIGE. SHE is also on the
     telephone.*)

PAIGE. Hey, Barbie, this is Paige. Can you
talk? ...

ROSEANNE. William doesn't come home
anymore. He doesn't like it here. With me, I
mean. He ignores me for hours some nights ...

PAIGE. Now do I care what *she* thinks? Did
you pick her? Did you have any input whatsoever
into what kind of a shithead you were going to get
for a roommate? ...

ROSEANNE. There are a couple of women
from the church I could talk to but they're both so
busy with their kids and their meetings ...

PAIGE. See, I never understood the logic to
that anyway. Throwing complete strangers
together who might be just so totally incompatible.
. . .

ROSEANNE. Well, there *is* Verdra. She's about the closest I'm ever going to come to having a best friend. ...

PAIGE. And like Chrissy and Serena. ...

ROSEANNE. Verdra lives in a mobile home park. She has no phone.

PAIGE. And the two Lindas.

ROSEANNE. How can anybody *exist* without a telephone?

PAIGE. And you look at Sissy and Tanya. ... Tanya. Tanya Merrick. (*SHE traces a line across her forehead with her index finger.*) Single eyebrow. Right. Sissy is like *very* religious. She even holds these prayer meetings in the room. I mean one time these two old ladies showed up in the dorm wearing their orthopedic shoes and carrying their big, bulging purses, and Tanya just stayed in the bathroom the whole time, flushing the toilet until they had to leave because of the noise.

(*LIGHTS come up in Dust's living space. DUST is on the phone.*)

DUST. (*Into phone.*) I am your sunshine. I am your moonglow. I am the light of amor which cannot be extinguished. And what are *you*, my pet? ... Wait. I didn't catch all of — ... You are the may — what? You are the mayfly which flutters fleetingly away — fleeing my soul. What does that mean? Hello? Hello?

PAIGE. Okay. His name is Trey Foster. ...
Fifteen minutes ago at Burger King. There is
power there, Barbie — real power in the way he
looks at me. Only one way to describe him — he is
a Viking. He is a reincarnated Viking warrior!

DUST. (*The phone still pressed to her ear.*)
No, I do not hear a dial tone. I hear the pulse of our
relationship beating vigorously with promise.

PAIGE. He was sitting there looking at me
with those blue Nordic eyes, and I felt like I'd died
and gone to heav— ... yeah, yeah, Valhalla —
whatever. And what's *really* incredible is — it
wasn't even an hour ago I was on the phone with
my sister Aneece, telling her about all the rotten
luck I've been having lately. So what happens? I
go down for a mustard Whopper and in walks
Thor the Magnificent! (*Apparently answering the
question: "What did you say his name was
again?"*) Trey. Trey Foster. Why? Do you know
him?

ROSEANNE. I'm telling you it's no use going
to my minister. He wouldn't counsel me. I'm his
wife!

(*AUDREY is now illuminated. SHE is also on the
telephone, this time without Rothschild at her
side.*)

AUDREY. (*Angry, upset.*) I don't understand.
We signed a two week contract. First
performance tonight at eight. You can't just — ...

(*SHE begins to pace nervously back and forth carrying the phone with her.*) Whose decision was that? ... Then let me talk to *him*.

(*LIGHTS come up on ANEECE talking on her phone.*)

ANEECE. Hello, Charlotte? I'm going to be a little late. Just hold my seat at the banquet table. It's my mother. She's sick, I think. I can't seem to get through to anyone to find out.

DUST. Yes, operator. I think we were disconnected. I was talking to someone and then suddenly he wasn't there anymore ... What do you mean "Did he have reason to terminate the call?"

AUDREY. Which Mr. Grubbs is this? The fat one or the skinny one? I want the Mr.Grubbs who booked me and Rothschild at your Reba's Rendezvous Lounge for the next two weeks.

DUST. "Did he say goodbye?" What are you — some kind of comedienne?

(*During Audrey's talk with Mr. Grubbs, ANEECE will end her phone conversation with Charlotte, try one last time to reach one of her sisters, then hang up and exit her bedroom.*)

AUDREY. Hello, yourself. Is this the Mr. Grubbs who walks with a limp? ... This is Audrey Hart of Hart and Rothschild. Why are you

yanking our act? ... We signed a contract. ...
Okay, *I* signed the contract. His fingers don't
work. ... No, I *won't* do the routine topless. My
husband would kill me. And you. *And* your fat
brother with the limp. Harry's an expert
marksman. We'd all be dead in a second. (*An
idea.*) Now wait a minute there. What if half the
act went topless? I'm sure Rothschild wouldn't
mind. All we got to do is paint some nipples and a
little belly button on him. He'd look like a real
little boy. ... What did I say that was so funny?
(*Angrily.*) Let me talk to Reba. ... Reba! ...
Reba's a *what?* Whose old coon dog? Never mind.
You'll be hearing from my lawyer in the
morning. (*SHE slams the phone down and grabs
the directory. SHE riffles through the yellow
pages; to herself:*) Lawyers – See attorneys.

PAIGE. (*Into phone.*) Something wonderful is
going to happen between us, Barb. You get that
feeling – once in maybe 150 guys you get that
special feeling.

AUDREY. (*To herself, as SHE dials.*)
Topless? Of all the nerve – signing a two week –
(*Into phone.*) Hello? I saw your ad in the yellow
pages. You look very handsome, like my husband
Harry. You look like you could really help
someone with legal – ... Who is this then? ... All
right. When will Big John Roberts be back in? ...
I'll have to call back. I'll be out all day Monday
and I don't have an answering machine. Harry
won't buy one because he says little kids just call

you up and go — (*Makes a raspberry.*) into the phone and you come home all tired at night and have to listen to this long string of — (*Three raspberries.*) See, I'll be auditioning on Monday. I'm a ventriloquist. Did you know that last year a ventriloquist made it to the finals of the Miss America Pageant? And her little boy was not nearly as clever as my little Rothschild.

(*ROSEANNE opens the cabinet door and pulls out a roll of paper towels. SHE tears one off and blows her nose.*)

ROSEANNE. (*Into phone.*) You're a good listener. Would you like to be my sister? (*A pause.*) Or brother?

(*Total BLACKOUT. A MUSICAL INTERLUDE carries us a few hours ahead to very early SATURDAY MORNING. LIGHTS come up slightly and remain dim in each of the six areas of the stage. PAIGE, ANEECE, AUDREY and DUST are asleep; PAIGE and ANEECE in their beds, DUST on her floor among her throw pillows, AUDREY in her armchair with a* Redbook Magazine *opened in her lap. Rothschild, his eyes closed, sits on the arm of the chair. ROSEANNE sits in the semi-darkness of her kitchen with her back to the audience. SHE is still dressed in what she had worn earlier in the evening. The phone*

*receiver is still pressed to her ear. Only one
thing has changed since we last saw her; SHE
is now surrounded by small hillocks of
discarded paper towel wads. PEGGY, now
wearing a nightgown, is sitting in a rocking
chair near the writing table. Lingeringly
SHE turns the pages of a photo album; SHE
seems lost in her memories. ANEECE's sleep
becomes restless. SHE wakes and sits up in
bed. SHE stares ahead, thinking. After a
moment SHE gets out of bed and pours herself
a drink.)*

PAIGE. (*Talking in her sleep.*) Yes. It's a
beautiful helmet. Are those real horns?

(*DUST awakes in the midst of a dream. SHE
reaches for her tape recorder which lies on the
floor nearby.*)

DUST. (*Trying to recall the dream she was
just having; into recorder:*) I am standing —
(*Yawns.*) I am standing in a field of clover.
Marching toward me is a company of uniformed
soldiers all of whom look like — (*Trying to
remember.*) — look like Bobby Charles Boulder
who took me to the Junior Prom. They carry their
rifles in one hand and their boxes of Stridex
Medicated Pads in the other. They come to a halt a
few yards away. Music plays. It is a disco tune.
We all dance. "You're very good, Bobby," I say.

"Thank you," the soldiers answer in unison. Then we all make love.

(*SHE sets the tape recorder down and falls back to sleep among the pillows. ROSEANNE nows shifts her position so we can see her face. SHE has been crying and dabs at her nose with one of the paper towels in her hand.*)

ROSEANNE. (*Into phone.*) Then for our last anniversary William bought me a book of verse and scriptures called *For Solace When He Has Gone Away*. I wouldn't even open it up. I thought it was about death. Turns out, it's for wives who are facing separation from their husbands. This was William's wonderful way of telling me how things are going between us. I'm sure he'd love to divorce me in a New York minute if he didn't have the board of stewards to answer to. So he stays away as much as he can. He doesn't fix my blender. He's stopped making love to me. (*SHE glances up at the clock.*) You know, you've been a saint to listen to me all this time. I wish I could meet you. ... Yes, I would imagine that preserving your anonymity *is* – ... Yes. Tomorrow I *will* call one of my sisters. Maybe I just never let them know how bad things have been going for me these last few weeks. One out of five sisters, surely – ... Yes. Thank you so much. Goodbye.

(*ROSEANNE hangs up, gathers up the strewn paper towel wads and deposits them in the trash canister, then stretches and walks slowly out of the kitchen, turning off the LIGHT on the way out.*)

PAIGE. (*Still talking in her sleep.*) And what do you do on weekends when you're *not* out raping and pillaging?

(*AUDREY wakes up, looks at her watch, then at Rothschild.*)

AUDREY. Come on, Roth. It's way past your bedtime.

(*SHE picks up Rothschild and carries him sleepily out of the room. ANEECE returns to bed. SHE lies back, closing her eyes. All LIGHTS fade out except those in Peggy's sitting room. PEGGY reaches a certain page and stops.*)

PEGGY. And that's all there is, Vincent. You stop right there. Didn't even make it through one complete photo album. What am I supposed to do with the rest of these pages?

(*The phone RINGS. It startles HER. SHE looks at her watch, turns and eyes the phone curiously.*

SHE walks slowly over and picks up the handset. Very evenly at first:)

PEGGY. Hello? ... No. I don't think I would like that. I think it would hurt. ... No, I don't think I like the sound of that either. May I go now? ... You know, you don't catch people in the best of moods when you call at three in the morning. Most people are in their deepest stage of sleep by three. Wouldn't you be a little impolite if somebody woke *you* from a deep sleep? ... Why don't you try warm milk or counting sheep? ... Yes, you could count those too, but I don't see how a parade of naked mamas is going to – ... No, actually you didn't have the pleasure. I was wide awake. I'm an insomniac probably just like you except that when *I* can't sleep, I just wander around all night *alone*. I don't resort to calling people on the phone to describe how I'd like to– You know, it takes an infantile mind to– ... I said you were not very bright, little boy. Nor articulate. You've used that same word ten times already. (*Losing composure.*) You're a very lucky man, little boy. If you had made this call two years ago, my husband would have been on the extension. He would have been listening to how you wanted to do this and that to various parts of my anatomy and he would have come looking for you. No place would have been safe. He would have found you out and ripped your voice box right out of your throat. Then you'd have to translate your filthy fantasies into sign language. And you know what? Sign language doesn't go over too well on the telephone. (*Answering a question.*) He died, you little creep. He got sick and died. It was the only battle he ever — (*SHE stops herself.*) I have some advice for you, little boy. Go into mommy and daddy's medicine cabinet and find the sleeping pills. Count out forty. Swallow. Pleasant dreams. (*SHE hangs up, turns to the photo album and tears out the blank pages. SHE drops them into a wastepaper basket.*) Now, Vincent, there *are* no empty pages.

(*SHE tucks the album under her arm and walks out of the room. LIGHTS fade out until the room is immersed again in darkness. A MUSICAL INTERLUDE takes us to later SATURDAY MORNING. LIGHTS come up in Peggy's sitting room — empty at present — and Aneece's bedroom. ANEECE sits on the edge of her bed. SHE dials her phone. Peggy's phone rings. PEGGY hurries in, wearing a robe.*)

PEGGY. (*Answering.*) Hello?
ANEECE. (*Unfriendly.*) I called back last night. Busy. A second time. Busy. A third time. No answer.
PEGGY. We left the house for a while. Mama wanted to play bingo.

ANEECE. That was the all important news —
that you and Mama were going out for an evening
of bingo?

PEGGY. No. Mama had gotten sick. There
was something wrong with the tuna.

ANEECE. *Tuna?*

PEGGY. (*Defensively.*) I had to take her to the
hospital, Aneece.

ANEECE. Was that on the way to the bingo
parlor?

PEGGY. I'm never to call you about Mama?

ANEECE. Christ, Peggy. Her partials fall out
in church and you dash to the phone to share it with
all of us. Her bowel movements become less
regular and it's back to the damn telephone.

PEGGY. (*Sullenly.*) You've made your point.

ANEECE. Don't you ever wonder why I moved
to Philadelphia?

PEGGY. You were offered a job there.

ANEECE. I was offered jobs in other places
too, Peggy. Better pay. Better perks. But you know
why I took the one in Philadelphia? One reason:
distance. It was about as far away as I could get
from Mama. From everything about that woman
that drives me up the wall.

PEGGY. Then I won't call you anymore. You
win.

ANEECE. That's not what I want.

PEGGY. Of course it is. You'd like to just
pretend she doesn't exist.

ANEECE. (*Rattled.*) No, Peggy. I just want you to start using a little goddamn discretion!

PEGGY. (*Almost whining.*) I assume I have your permission to call if she dies. Maybe if I keep it short and sweet: "Hello, Aneece. Mama's dead. If you care to send flowers —"

ANEECE. (*Laughing mordantly.*) That woman's going to outlive us all.

PEGGY. She's had congestive heart failure twice this year.

ANEECE. It was bronchitis. Mild bronchitis.

PEGGY. That was last year. And it wasn't mild.

ANEECE. All right, Peggy. I will concede the fact that Mama has respiratory problems. But people with respiratory problems have been known to live to be very old.

PEGGY. And the accidents. You can't discount all the freak accidents.

ANEECE. Last month you called to tell me Mama tripped on a squirrel. You had me called out of an important meeting — and how the hell you got put through to the conference room I'll never know.

PEGGY. I told them it was an emergency.

ANEECE. You told them — ? Well, it *wasn't* an emergency, Peggy. Not even for the squirrel. Mama fall down. Mama go boom. Mama get up. Nothing broken.

PEGGY. We did not know that at the time. Her leg swelled up so badly.

ANEECE. Peggy, Mama's going to keep tripping on squirrels. She's going to keep eating contaminated food. I'll *even* bet you that somewhere out there lurks another crazed woman who's going to mistake Mama for Loretta Young and chase her around the perfume counter at Goldsmith's Department Store. Because you know what, Peggy? Our mother is unlucky. But there's not a damn thing in the world I can do about that and I'm just sick to death of hearing about it. We all have better things to do than listen to Mama's little misadventures two and three times a week.

PEGGY. What do you mean by "we"? You think Roseanne and Audrey feel about her the way you do? You think they hate her too?

ANEECE. I don't hate Mama. I just won't canonize her the way you have.

PEGGY. I need to go.

ANEECE. Time to pull Mama's frail body out of bed for breakfast?

PEGGY. It just so happens, Aneece, that Mama is usually the first one up. Last night, though, she must have slept wrong or something. She can't move her neck.

ANEECE. (*Laughing.*) Food poisoning, then the old cement neck. Still I'd say this has been one of her better weeks.

PEGGY. I'm going, Aneece.

ANEECE. (*Softening a bit.*) Look, Peggy. I know how much you love her. And I know —

PEGGY. (*Interrupting.*) We all love her —
with one exception.

ANEECE. We have lives beyond that old
house in midtown Memphis, Peggy. Mama's not
the centerpiece anymore.

PEGGY. You can't discard her that easily.

ANEECE. I'm not discarding her. I'm getting
some distance. For my sanity.

PEGGY. Then I meant what I said. I'll stop
calling you.

ANEECE. (*Wearily.*) You do whatever you
want.

PEGGY. (*After a beat.*) I can't make you love
her, can I?

ANEECE. I told you, Peggy. I don't hate
Mama.

PEGGY. But I don't think you love her. Prove
me wrong, Aneece. Say you love her. Say it.

ANEECE. (*After a long pause.*) It would only
be words.

(*PEGGY hangs up. Both LIGHTS fade as EACH
WOMAN sits staring at her telephone. As
darkness envelopes them, LIGHTS come up
on PAIGE and DUST. BOTH are on the phone,
PAIGE lying in bed wearing a long
University of Texas jersey used as a
nightshirt and munching from a bag of potato
chips; DUST sitting yoga-style on the floor in
her leotards, a bowl of cereal beside her.*)

PAIGE. But why "Dust?" Colander made more sense.

DUST. When I embraced the name last week I felt like one of those tiny particles of dust that dance in the sunshafts. A minuscule speck suddenly brought to light as dawn peeks through the window.

PAIGE. And what do you feel like today?

DUST. A homeless collie dog. Call me Shannon, Dog of the Moors.

PAIGE. I caught you at a bad time.

DUST. True. But I've still got a clear head. I never let hate or sorrow or jealousy take my brain hostage.

PAIGE. Well, I need some advice.

DUST. Shoot.

PAIGE. Nothing's wrong, mind you. In fact, I'm really kind of excited about the whole thing. See, I've got this date with a Viking. I mean that's the only way I can describe him. Now I never thought I'd be asking this with all of my experience —

DUST. I'm one step ahead of you, little sister. It's the old "How do I let him know how I feel without letting him know how I feel?" dilemma. Yes, Paige, Shannon, Dog of the Moors has walked down *that* country road before.

PAIGE. This time it feels really special. I don't want to screw it up.

DUST. Like poor Shannon.

PAIGE. What did *she* do?

DUST. The poor dear opened her heart to someone who was repulsed by the sight of blood.

PAIGE. I can't understand you when you talk figuratively.

DUST. (*Translating.*) I told the guy I loved him. Then he dumped me.

PAIGE. Who was it? Carter?

DUST. No. Carter rejoined the circus last month. This new one I called "Chore Boy." He did odd jobs for me. I pretended his services were adequate. Never tipped *too* much. Until two nights ago. I got very drunk.

PAIGE. Drunk on his affection?

DUST. No. Drunk on Tequila Sunrises. I said things – things which unveiled my soul.

PAIGE. Like what?

DUST. Like "I worship you. I want to pray to you."

PAIGE. You blew it.

DUST. I got too close, Paige, and now he wants his freedom. He calls himself "Mayfly." I think he's more like the honeybee.

PAIGE. Because he stung you, right?

DUST. No.

PAIGE. No?

DUST. No, Paige. The honeybee – he's always buzzing from flower to flower, never tarrying too long at any one blossom. Maybe he thinks it will start to wither. I suppose in my love's eyes I began to wither.

PAIGE. I've never really had to worry about that before. I guess to most guys I'm like — (*Thinking up the right analogy.*) — a flowering evergreen tree!

DUST. Until the Viking came along. Don't go singing your siren song too loudly, Paige dear, or the 'ol Norseman will just plug up his ears and move on to the next wench.

PAIGE. What's a wench?

DUST. It's a hoisting machine.

PAIGE. (*After a moment's thought.*) Yeah. Okay.

DUST. I shall go now. I have to get to the market before they run out of carob powder and stone ground wheat flour.

PAIGE. Before you go — Aneece said something was wrong with Mama. Did Peggy call you?

DUST. Mama's okay. Some bad squid or something. I think they pumped her stomach a couple of times.

PAIGE. Okay, then. I'll let you go.

DUST. *Au Revoir, ma petite soeur.*

PAIGE. 'Bye.

(*PAIGE hangs up. As the LIGHTS in Paige's dorm room fade out, DUST speaks to the telephone.*)

DUST. Good luck with Eric the Red.

(*The LIGHTS in Dust's room fade out as well.
LIGHTS come up in Audrey's den. AUDREY
is on the phone, a pad and pencil in her hand.
Rothschild is not with her.*)

AUDREY. (*Extremely distressed.*) Yes. I
want the number for the sheriff's office in
Bucking Horse. I think it's in Missouri. In the
Ozarks. You know — the Ozark Mountains. My
husband is there. He's on a hunting trip and I
desperately need to talk to him. ... No, I don't
know what county it's in. Don't you have an atlas
or something? ... Maybe there's a forest ranger's
post around there somewhere. ... Then what about
Arkansas? Maybe it's in Arkansas. I've never
been there, miss. I don't go with Harry on his
hunting and fishing trips. I don't like guns or
live bait ... You don't understand. This is a dire
emergency. My son is gone. Someone has
abducted my little boy and I have to talk to Harry.
... I've already dialed 911. The police won't help
me because my boy is wooden. ... Yes. He's made
of wood. ... No, his name is not Pinocchio! ...
This is not a prank call. I want my boy back,
damn it! Wait! Don't — Please don't — (*Defeated,
SHE lets her phone hand drop limply to her side.*)
Hang up. (*SHE begins to cry. SHE picks up one of
the hunting trophies and speaks to it.*) Where are
you when I need you, Harry? How important can
it be stalking the wild game with Amos — driving
four hundred miles from home to shoot at little

creatures that never did *you* any harm, while our little Rothschild is out there in the clutches of God only knows what kind of a pervert, and I can't even get you on the damn telephone. Don't you even care, Harry? You created him, for God's sake. You put him together with your own two hands. You did such a damn good job. Too good.

(*The LIGHTS in her den fade as those in Aneece's bedroom come up. ANEECE is sitting on the bed talking on the phone.*)

ANEECE. Hello, Ms. James, this is Aneece Walker. ... Yes, I was wondering if Dr. Meyer held sessions on Saturdays. I know I just started seeing him last month, and I certainly realize I'm not among that inner core of patients who date back to his early years right out of Penn. On the other hand, I lost an awful lot of ground when Dr. Elam retired. Dr. Meyer and I have made great strides in our first four sessions, but Ms. James, there are some things I *must* discuss with him that can't possibly wait until Tuesday. ... Certainly it's not *that* grave. I just wondered if Meyer had a few minutes ... Yes, I'll hold.

(*We leave ANEECE holding. LIGHTS come up on DUST sitting on the floor with the phone to her ear.*)

DUST. (*Into phone.*) I want to talk – (*A deep breath.*) I want to talk to Chore Boy. ... Wait. Don't hang up. I also call him Mayfly. ... No, this is not a joke. I don't know his real name. That's part of the problem. Maybe I can describe him to you.

(*LIGHTS come back up in Paige's dorm room. The phone RINGS. PAIGE enters, now wearing jeans and a sweat shirt.*)

PAIGE. (*Answering.*) Hello? ... Yes it is. ... Is that *you*, Barbie? This is not funny. ... I'm going to hang up. I mean it. ... What about Trey Foster? (*Listens with total disbelief.*) You're crazy – a complete looney tune, you know it?

DUST. Hello, Frank. The name really fits you. Look, I have reconciled myself to the fact that it is over between us. You've got a global-sized garden out there to pollinate. I accept that. But I do not wish us to part as jaded lovers. You're right that life is much too short. Every moment must be seized and put to good use. Savored, learned from, spent nurturing others. I wanted to nurture you, Frank. I loved you. I have that in me. I am a Walker woman. ... A *Walker* woman! ... No, no. I mean my last name is Walker. What I'm trying to say, Frank, is – I'm too much like my sisters. I won't deny it. Men play a big part in our lives. (*A sigh.*) There now. I've said it. I must admit this has all been very therapeutic. And now

I bid you a fond — (*Stops; Frank has apparently interrupted her. SHE smiles.*) Of course there are always a few chores left undone. You want to earn a little Coca Cola money? (*HER smile broadens as LIGHTS fade out.*)

PAIGE. (*Very agitated.*) Are you finished? ... Because I can see straight through your sick little scheme, Miss Barbie Grinder. You say these things about Trey so I won't go out with him and then you step in, shake your fat butt and you two ride off into the sunset together. True friend you are. Where were you when I really needed you, *friend?* When I couldn't get that oily Leonard Mueller to stop sending me love letters he'd signed with his own blood or whatever the hell was dripping all over the stationery. Well your plan just isn't going to work, Barbie. And by the way — you do a shitty job of disguising your voice. Your R's still sound like L's. (*SHE slams the phone handset into its cradle, then quickly yanks it back up and dials a number SHE has written on her hand. Into phone:*) Is this Cindy Blackstone? ... Somebody told me I should call you. They say you went out with Trey Foster a couple of times. ... So tell me — is he gay? (*A frown comes across her face as SHE listens.*) Okay, like how gay is he? ... Because I think I'm in love with him, that's why. ... Well, hoe your own long row, you bitch!

(*SHE hangs up, then boots the phone off the bed. Total BLACKOUT. MUSIC plays. We move*

*ahead to late SATURDAY NIGHT. LIGHTS
come up on ROSEANNE who sits perched on
her kitchen counter staring at the telephone. It
RINGS. SHE pounces on it.)*

ROSEANNE. William? ... Where *are* you?
I've been worried. ... It's almost midnight.
Tomorrow's Sunday. Have you prepared your—
(*Interrupted.*) But you've been spending so much
time at Bud's. Why don't you come on home? We
can talk about it. ... Something's happening to our
marriage, William. The girls, they ask me
questions I can't answer: "Why is Daddy so quiet
all the time?", "Where is Daddy? When is he
coming home?" You know what I should do,
William? I should stand up in front of the
congregation and tell them about you. It would
knock them right out of their pews. If you don't
love me anymore, then why in Heaven's name
don't you say it? (*SHE listens for a long time,
fighting back the tears; then with bitter sarcasm:*)
Thank you, dear. Thank you for coming right out
with it. (*SHE hangs up; bravely:*) First take three
deep breaths. (*SHE takes three very exaggerated
deep breaths.*) Next, talk to someone. Anyone. Do
not keep it inside. (*SHE picks up the phone.*) Who
am I calling? (*SHE hangs up and stares blankly
at the various condiments gathered on her
counter. SHE picks up the ketchup bottle. An
imagined telephone conversation:*) Hello,
Aneece. This is Roseanne. (*Pause.*) Your sister!

Say, Aneece, my marriage seems to be falling apart. Do you have a minute? (*Playing the part of Aneece.*) I'm sorry, Roseanne, but I'm just not interested in your petty marital problems. I am making money. I am making too much money to be bothered by you. (*ROSEANNE looks seethingly at the ketchup bottle for a moment, then slings it to the floor. It shatters. SHE addresses what remains of the ketchup bottle:*) You can't make any more money now, Aneece. You're dead. (*SHE now pulls out the pepper shaker.*) Hello? Is Paige there? (*Pause.*) Yes, well, when her blow dryer is repaired and she's ready to come out of seclusion, tell her that her sister Roseanne called. (*SHE tosses the pepper shaker aside, then grabs up the sugar bowl.*) Sherry, this is Roseanne. Can you come down from the planet Zimzax for a few minutes? (*As DUST, between tokes on an imaginary joint.*) Roseanne? Hmmmm. I don't think I know a Roseanne. Your voice sounds familiar though. Sounds like Preacherwife. That you, Preacherwife? What's wrong with the marriage, babe? Tired of the missionary position? (*SHE dumps the sugar bowl and extracts a bottle of steak sauce.*) Audrey? No, wait! Don't put the dummy on! (*SHE "hangs up" on Audrey and picks up the salt shaker.*) Hello, Peggy. Salt of the earth. Looks like you win by default.

*(LIGHTS fade out as ROSEANNE goes to the
telephone. MUSIC comes up.)*

END OF ACT I

ACT II

LIGHTS come up on: ROSEANNE standing at her kitchen counter, the telephone receiver to her ear, the salt shaker in one hand. The phone RINGS in Peggy's sitting room as LIGHTS fade up there. PEGGY has been washing dishes and drys her hands with a dishcloth on her way to the phone.

PEGGY. Hello?

ROSEANNE. Peggy, this is Roseanne. Did I wake you?

PEGGY. No. I was up. What is it?

ROSEANNE. Things aren't going too well. What if I came home for a couple of days — maybe brought the girls?

PEGGY. Mama would love that.

ROSEANNE. And you — *you'd* be glad to see me, too?

PEGGY. Of course I would.

ROSEANNE. I know I've never been your favorite sister.

PEGGY. I've never played favorites, Roseanne.

ROSEANNE. (*Trying to make a joke.*) You hate us all.

PEGGY. (*Playfully.*) Yes. I hate you all equally.

ROSEANNE. I sometimes wonder, though, if there are times you don't wish one of us were still in Memphis. Especially after Vincent died and Mama asked you to move in with her.

PEGGY. Moving in with Mama was *my* decision, Rose. And I'm glad I can be here to help her.

ROSEANNE. Peggy – (*SHE stops.*)

PEGGY. What is it? What's the matter?

ROSEANNE. I need you to help me sort things out.

PEGGY. You don't sound good at all.

ROSEANNE. My icemaker is on the fritz. The cubes are coming out all deformed looking. And it rained all last week and it was so dark around here I had to turn on every light in the house. And just now – just now William told me he doesn't love me anymore. He said it on the phone. He doesn't even have the guts to tell me to my face.

PEGGY. You need to talk to Mama about this.

ROSEANNE. I don't want her to know about it just now. You know how she worries about things.

PEGGY. You know – I could have been a better sister to you, Rose. I didn't protect you from the others the way I should have. Remember the Christmas we all exchanged names? I should have made it my duty to find out who drew yours. Who bought you the eighty-nine cent Lifesavers storybook. I should have shamed them into returning it and getting you the doll you wanted. But I didn't do it.

ROSEANNE. Why?

PEGGY. I don't remember. (*SHE thinks a moment.*) Maybe I thought you had no use for a doll with interchangeable heads.

ROSEANNE. (*Laughing.*) Afraid I might be turning into another Sherry?

PEGGY. (*Also laughing.*) One space queen in the family was enough. By the way — she's calling herself "Dust" this week.

ROSEANNE. Dust? What happened to "Naomi the Shepherdess?"

PEGGY. (*Teasingly.*) Good Lord, Rose. That was five or six names ago. Don't you two stay in touch?

ROSEANNE. Last August she gave me one of her couscous recipes. William and the girls had stomach cramps for two days.

PEGGY. (*A thought.*) Aneece drew your name that Christmas, didn't she?

ROSEANNE. I don't have positive proof, but I did notice she had a little extra money for the movies that week.

PEGGY. Come see us. It's been ages.

ROSEANNE. Does Mama still snore?

PEGGY. (*Laughing.*) Worse than ever. Some nights it's like sleeping next to a working construction site.

ROSEANNE. In the oddest kind of way I miss that sound. Our house is so quiet at night. I should have had six daughters instead of two.

PEGGY. What? And increase the odds of getting a Sherry or an Aneece?

ROSEANNE. (*Feigned protest.*) Peggy!

(*LIGHTS go out over both PEGGY and ROSEANNE, and come up on AUDREY and ANEECE, also on the phone. AUDREY sits in her chair; ANEECE lies draped over her bed, a glass of something in her hand.*)

AUDREY. I called Roseanne and I called Peggy but their lines were busy — and Sherry wasn't in. At least that's what I think her answering machine was trying to tell me. It said something like "There is no dust in this house tonight. It has been swept clean by the magic broom of a chore boy."

ANEECE. (*Drunk but not exaggeratedly so.*) Our sister should have been committed years ago.

AUDREY. So I called *you*.

ANEECE. This means I'm number four on your list?

AUDREY. No. It's just that I know how busy you always are.

ANEECE. You know what I'm doing right now?

AUDREY. Probably looking over briefs.

ANEECE. No, Audrey. Lawyers look over briefs. Commercial loan officers do not look over briefs. No, right now I am attempting to polish off a whole bottle of vodka in one sitting. I have no doubt that I shall succeed.

AUDREY. (*Innocently.*) Are you having a party, Aneece?

ANEECE. (*Sarcastically.*) Yeah. I'm having a blast.

AUDREY. I won't bother you anymore. I'll call Paige.

ANEECE. You won't get Paige. It's Saturday night. She's out screwing the University of Texas. The kid's got it down to a science. She starts by passing out condoms stamped with her name and phone number.

AUDREY. Are you ill, Aneece?

ANEECE. I'm swacked. I am good and swacked. My analyst dropped me today. He said I was crazy.

AUDREY. I lost Rothschild this morning.

ANEECE. I didn't know you had a dog.

AUDREY. I don't. Rothschild was my wooden boy. Harry created him for me in his woodworking shop.

ANEECE. You lost your *dummy?*

AUDREY. Someone took him. I set him on a bar stool at this club in Jackson and I went back to talk to the manager in his office. When I came out Rothschild was gone. All that was left was his little dickey. (*SHE takes the dickey out of her pocket and looks at it.*)

ANEECE. His little what?

AUDREY. Dickey.

ANEECE. (*Becoming very interested.*) Nobody saw it happen?

AUDREY. I don't know. I asked the bartender. He just made a joke out of it. He said Rothschild had asked for a wine cooler and then the bartender says, "We don't serve drinks to dummies like you." So Rothschild just hopped down off the stool and marched off in a huff.

ANEECE. But his legs don't work.

AUDREY. Of course they don't work. That's why the joke wasn't very funny. On stage when I sit him up on my knee those little spindly legs just dangle there kind of lifelessly like he had polio.

ANEECE. Did you call the police?

AUDREY. They wouldn't help me.

ANEECE. What did Harry do?

AUDREY. He doesn't know about it. He won't be home until tomorrow night.

ANEECE. I'm really sorry, Audrey. I mean one minute he's there on a barstool safe and sound — the next minute you're saying goodbye to both your career *and* your firstborn.

AUDREY. You're making fun of me, aren't you?

ANEECE. (*Sincerely.*) No, Audrey.

AUDREY. (*Hurt.*) I knew it was a mistake to call you.

ANEECE. I was *not* being facetious, Audrey.

AUDREY. I don't hear a party. You're all alone, aren't you? You're drinking there all alone like an alcoholic.

ANEECE. I *am* an alcoholic.

AUDREY. Then you need help.

ANEECE. Not interested.

AUDREY. I want Harry to talk to you about AA.

ANEECE. Don't you dare start up with the —

AUDREY. You need help. Harry got help.

ANEECE. I don't need AA, Audrey. Not AA or Triple A or anything else that goes by some bouncy little acronym and shoves you a happy helping hand. I've had my fill of helping hands. Of analysts and group therapy sessions and people who think *they* alone can help you look inside yourself and pull out all the answers. If I want to flounder, it's nobody's goddamn business.

AUDREY. We're still going to worry about you, Aneece. You think we can just cut it off?

ANEECE. I wish to God you could.

AUDREY. You need to go home for a while and see everybody.

ANEECE. I don't care to go home, Audrey. I don't feel about home the way the rest of you do.

AUDREY. This thing between you and Mama just goes on and on.

ANEECE. She doesn't even call me, Audrey. She won't even pick up the damn telephone and make one simple call.

AUDREY. She doesn't touch the phone. She doesn't call *anyone.*

ANEECE. (*Having fun at Audrey's expense.*) Why, Audrey? I'd love to hear you say it.

AUDREY. You *know* why.

ANEECE. No, Audrey. I want to hear *you* say it.

AUDREY. (*Coldly.*) You're really getting a kick out of this, aren't you?

ANEECE. You bet I am. I go into absolute hysterics when I think about why our mother — (*SHE explodes into uncontrollable laughter. Struggling to produce the words:*) It's the possibility of lightning, Audrey. Lightning traveling through the phone lines. (*As Mother.*) "It can happen. I wouldn't take that kind of risk with any of you girls. Why I wouldn't get on that instrument of death if the President himself was inviting me to a White House gala!"

AUDREY. (*Growing angry.*) We've lived with Mama's quirks for years. You think any of us love her less because she gets kooky sometimes?

ANEECE. Mama's a kook. This is great. One of you finally found the nerve to say what we've known all along. But don't stop there. Let's say what else she is.

AUDREY. You haven't seen her in years. When was the last time you went home?

ANEECE. We were at war with Germany!

AUDREY. It was for my wedding, wasn't it?

ANEECE. I don't remember.

AUDREY. That was seven years ago, Aneece. You haven't seen Mama in *seven years*?

(*ANEECE doesn't answer.*)

AUDREY. How will you live with yourself if she was to die before you went home?

ANEECE. (*Sarcastically.*) Hello, Peggy. When did *you* get on the line?

AUDREY. I worry about her too. Remember when her toenails started coming off for no reason?

ANEECE. Peggy and I already covered this ground a few hours ago. Sorry you missed it.

AUDREY. You're never going to forgive Mama for anything, are you?

ANEECE. Our childhood was one long horror movie, Audrey. How easy, or should I say *convenient* it's been for all of you to forget it.

AUDREY. I haven't forgotten. I remember what Daddy was. An alcoholic. Just like Harry is an alcoholic. Like *you* are an alcoholic.

ANEECE. I can't speak for Harry, sister, but *I* don't point guns at people when I get boozed up. I don't try to run over our mother in the driveway. I've never thrown Roseanne down the stairs or smashed the Christmas tree to bits because I thought my daughters were little shits who didn't deserve to celebrate Christmas. You want more?

AUDREY. (*Weakly.*) No.

ANEECE. Mama could have kicked dear old Dad's ass out of Memphis if she'd had the nerve. But she didn't . Mama was and still is a cowering and whining little mouse, and she permitted our father's reign of terror to continue unabated right up until the day God showed this family some long overdue mercy and struck him dead with a heart attack.

(*Long silence. LIGHTS come up in Paige's dormitory room. PAIGE enters, ecstatic. SHE leaps onto the bed, kicks off her shoes and lies back. SHE pulls the phone to her and balances it on her stomach. SHE dials.*)

PAIGE. (*Happily.*) Barbie Grinder please. ... No. I don't believe I'd like to call back. You be a good roommate and put Barbie on the phone. This is very important. (*Waits.*) Hi Barbie. This is Paige. But you may call me "The Miracle Worker." Yes, I went out with Gay Trey and I have news for you: Trey is gay no more. ... You got it. The right woman has transformed him into the red-blooded American male he was meant to be. *Total transformation,* Barbie. Like he'd just been waiting for someone like me to come along to deliver him. ... What's so funny? What's so damn funny?
AUDREY. Can I send you a pamphlet?
ANEECE. What kind of a pamphlet?

AUDREY. It's called "Coping." It's pretty good, Aneece. I read it twice this evening when I couldn't stop thinking about Rothschild.

ANEECE. I don't need anything put out by one of Harry's support groups.

AUDREY. That's not how I got it. I wrote to the Ask Amanda column in the paper. I asked her for six. One for me and one for each of my sisters.

ANEECE. (*Laughing derisively.*) You're incredible! You — are — *incredible!*

PAIGE. You stop laughing like that, you hear me? Stop it! Stop it!

(*Total BLACKOUT. MUSICAL INTERLUDE. It is now late morning/early afternoon on SUNDAY [depending on the time zone.] LIGHTS come up on ROSEANNE in her kitchen. SHE has not changed out of her church clothes.*)

ROSEANNE. (*Into phone, nervously.*) Hello, Bud. William missed church this morning. Everyone was concerned. I told them he was sick. That fat Mr. Haguewood from Haguewood Nurseries filled in with one of his off-the-cuff sermons about how mulching around a tree was like preparing for the Kingdom of God. Nobody got the connection and Brother Farrell shouted at him to sit down. (*A breath.*) Bud, I don't want you to ask him to the phone. Just tell me if he's all — (*Listens for a moment; a strange look comes over her face.*) I don't understand. Why would William – ... What am I supposed to do now, Bud? What do I do *now?*

(*LIGHTS fade out on ROSEANNE and come up on Dust's living space and Peggy's sitting room. DUST has dressed for the day. PEGGY is still in her robe. SHE sits in her rocking chair, reading the magazine section of the Sunday paper, a cup of coffee in her hand. DUST dials her phone. Peggy's phone RINGS.*)

PEGGY. (*Answering.*) Hello?

DUST. I greet you, sister Margaret.

PEGGY. Good morning, Sherry. No, it wasn't Sherry, was it? It was something like lust.

DUST. (*Curtly.*) Have you spoken to Roseanne lately?

PEGGY. Last night. Why?

DUST. Is she missing a husband by any chance?

PEGGY. What are you talking about?

DUST. A couple of hours ago someone showed up at my door. (*SHE cranes her head to look into an adjoining room.*) Someone who matches the description perfectly.

PEGGY. You're saying William is *there?*

DUST. My Mayfly left very early this morning to see the Grateful Dead revival in Portland and I went back to bed. Then along about eight – (*Melodramatically, à la Poe's* "The

Raven".) — as I nodded, nearly napping, suddenly there came a tapping, as of some preacher gently rapping, rapping at my kitchen door.

PEGGY. (*Impatiently.*) So William is there, Sherry?

DUST. Yes, Peggy. That's what I've been telling you.

PEGGY. (*Overlapping.*) My God.

DUST. Turned up on my doorstep like a little lost puppy. Told me he was taking his life in a new direction. He's giving up the ministry to travel the blue highways of America in a second-hand RV with his trusty cocker spaniel Benny at his side. We're going into Seattle this afternoon to look at RVs. Tomorrow I'm taking him to a pet shop to pick out Benny.

PEGGY. Why on earth would William go to *you* to work through his middle age crisis?

DUST. (*Having fun.*) Perhaps because I'm the only person he's ever met who entertains that impulse to break free of all of life's meaningless—

PEGGY. (*Interrupting, loudly.*) Or is it — (*Having silenced Dust, SHE now speaks in a normal tone.*) — because William has always had this thing for you?

DUST. (*A schoolgirl.*) Oh, you really think so?

PEGGY. Why else would he start his voyage of discovery in Seattle, of all places?

DUST. (*Scampishly.*) I don't know. The weather maybe?

PEGGY. (*Her temper rising.*) You know, Sherry, you are the most infuriating – William Johnson has been in love with you since the day Roseanne first brought him home to meet the family. And I haven't forgotten that he actually proposed to *you* before he proposed to *her*. You turned him down cold. You said you could never be a minister's wife because giving in to temptation was a habit you just weren't about to break.

DUST. (*First line spoken along with Peggy.*) – I just wasn't about to break. Good memory, dear Peg. So what are you worrying about? I've never had more than just a curious interest in William. Then and now. I just want to see that he gets a good send-off on his little blacktop adventure.

PEGGY. You're not going to mention Roseanne and the girls? You're just going to pretend they don't –

DUST. (*Breaking in.*) I won't lay that kind of guilt on him, Peggy. His conscience will begin working overtime soon enough. You know, William is not a man without some scruples.

PEGGY. (*Hesitantly.*) Did you – sleep with him?

DUST. My God, he's only been here two hours!

PEGGY. Are you *going* to sleep with him, Sherry?

DUST. Maybe. I told you, I'd like to give him a good send-off.

(*PEGGY doesn't reply.*)

DUST. That damn judgmental silence. I can just see that old school marm pout on your face.

(*Again, no retort from PEGGY.*)

DUST. Isn't this where you slam the receiver down with righteous indignation?

PEGGY. (*Slowly, burning.*) I won't hang up on you, Sherry. I assume you called me for a legitimate reason. You want me to phone Roseanne.

DUST. I don't think *I* should be the one to tell her.

PEGGY. Do I give her the truth or do you have any other suggestions?

DUST. The truth will do just fine. William is in Washington state for a few days and then he's driving down to San Francisco and L.A. Eventually, he'll make it back to Atlanta. And Roseanne will probably think he's gone off the deep end, which we all know he has, but it's okay because he's always wanted to know what the water felt like.

PEGGY. (*Without a smile.*) You could rationalize mass murder.

DUST. You expect too much out of people, Peggy. I've learned that humans are, by their nature, base and disgusting creatures. But now and then they do rise up from the muck and the mire and do something very humane. When this happens, it makes me very happy. When it doesn't, well, Peg – I just don't lose any sleep over it. Ciao!

(*SHE hangs up. Her LIGHTS fade out. PEGGY places the phone handset back in its cradle.*)

PEGGY. (*Rehearsing her conversation with Roseanne.*) Hello, Rose. Remember how William always wanted to see the Pacific Ocean?

(*Her LIGHTS also fade out. PAIGE is slowly illuminated, talking on the phone on the floor beside her bed.*)

PAIGE. (*Tense, with calculated politeness.*) Trey, this is Paige. Paige Walker. I wanted to talk to you about last night. I think I need to explain a few things. Last night, Trey, you only saw one side of me. I mean, there is so much more to Paige Walker than you – (*Interrupted, then brightly.*) That was a – very heterosexual thing to say. You're making great progress. ... Yeah, I'm free tonight. You know, to be honest with you, I'm not usually such a wild woman on the first date. It's just that I felt there were some things that

maybe you didn't know were out there. ... What
friends? ... Meet me? I'm flatter– ... Tonight
would be per– ... What do you mean I'm going to
be one fatigued sex kitten when these old Toms
say goodnight?

(*As LIGHTS in Paige's dorm room go out,
LIGHTS come up in Roseanne's kitchen.
ROSEANNE stands at her counter staring at a
bottle of Scotch and an empty glass. SHE picks
up the bottle and glass and pours herself a
drink. SHE considers the amount she has just
poured for a moment, then pours a little more.
Still not enough. SHE pours even more.
Finally satisfied that this is the "right
amount" SHE brings the glass slowly to her
lips and takes a big sip, then immediately
spits it out, spraying the kitchen.
BLACKOUT. MUSIC takes us forward to
SUNDAY NIGHT. A phone RINGS. LIGHTS
come up in Audrey's den. AUDREY runs in
and answers it.*)

AUDREY. Hello? (*Suddenly apprehensive.*)
Yes it is. ... What kind of an accident? (*HER face
registers terror.*) Oh, God, no. Is he hurt? Where
is– ... He broke his what? ... His tubula. What's a
– ... What's a perforated doodooum? Is that you,
Amos? ... Goddamn you, Amos. You scared the
crap out of me. Where is Harry? Put Harry on. (*A
pause.*) Was this your idea, Harry? (*Skeptical.*)

Sure. Sure. ... No, you don't have to sign anything in blood. I believe you. Where are you? ... Three hours to the promised land is still three hours too long, you old sugar bear. You just leave Amos in the rest room of that Stuckeys and high-tail it on home. ... Then say to him, "Amos, you're a cruel son of a bitch playing that kind of joke on my wife and if you don't straighten up, I'll shoot off your two big ears." ... I love you too, Harry.

(*As the LIGHTS in Audrey's den dim out, LIGHTS come up in Dust's living space. SHE is on the telephone.*)

DUST. Hi, Frank. This is the girl of your dreams. How was the concert? ... Let me share that feeling with you. (*SHE closes her eyes, throws her arms up in the air and gyrates for a few seconds. Back on the phone.*) Thank you, Frank. I love these little moments. Listen, the reason I called, I'm going down to Frisco with a friend of mine. He's really more family than friend — my brother-in-law. I'll be back in a week or so. I didn't want you to wonder where I'd — ... Well, aren't *you* the understanding one? Goodbye, my pet. (*SHE hangs up and starts out of the room. The telephone RINGS. Answering:*) I greet you. ... Hello, William. Where are you? I'm just about packed. You got that baby gassed up? ... But I thought we were going to California together. I thought you wanted a little company on the first

leg of your – ... *Human* company, William. ...
Of course I understand. You're a slave to your
impulses, and that inner voice is saying go it
alone. ... Then I wish you happiness, adventure,
and peace of mind. Godspeed to you. (*SHE hangs
up.*) You Bible-thumping little fart. (*SHE picks up
the phone and dials.*) Hello again, Frank. I've
decided I just *cannot* go off and leave this place
looking like Appalachia. Can you drop by this
evening and help me tidy up? Maybe later we can
work up a little sweat over at *your* sty. ... Good,
and wear those worn-out overalls – the ones with
all the holes. ... That's my boy.

(*LIGHTS fade out over DUST and come up over
ROSEANNE and PEGGY, both on the phone.*)

PEGGY.   Roseanne,   William's   in
Washington.
ROSEANNE. I know.
PEGGY. (*Surprised.*) You know?
ROSEANNE. I talked to Bud. He said
William was going to rent an RV and a dog. He
was going to "see what this great land is all
about." Can you really rent a dog, Peggy?
PEGGY. Are you okay?
ROSEANNE. No. (*A beat.*) But I'm better. I
tried to get drunk this afternoon but that didn't
work. Then I went down to the basement to find
William's antique revolver. I thought I might
blow my head off but I came across this pile of

dirty laundry beside the washer so I just got busy.
I turned on one of those talk radio shows and just
threw myself into washing and drying and the
civil rights of transvestites. Did you know three of
our presidents were cross dressers?

PEGGY. William will come home,
Roseanne. He'll start to miss you and the girls.

ROSEANNE. Maybe Melissa and Melanie.
He won't miss *me*.

PEGGY. Why do you do that to yourself?

ROSEANNE. It's just a fact. There never was
that much love between William and me. I
wanted him because I wanted a family and he was
so different from Daddy. I felt safe with William.
And I suppose he wanted *me* because I was
probably the only girl he knew who said she
wouldn't mind life in the fishbowl — people
always looking in at you to make sure you're
living clean and respectable lives like a
preacher's family should. At least now we're out
of the fishbowl.

PEGGY. I spoke to Sherry.

ROSEANNE. I guess she's taking good care of
him. Feeding him right and all that. He gets
chronic gas with the wrong kind of diet. For ten
years we lived in fear he'd have an attack behind
the pulpit and they'd have to evacuate the church!
(*ROSEANNE and PEGGY laugh.*) Of course now
it doesn't matter. On the road with a dog, you can
just poot and toot to your heart's content.

(LIGHTS come up on Paige's dorm room. PAIGE sits on her bed, holding the telephone in her lap. SHE dials a number from a slip of paper in her hand.)

ROSEANNE. Did you tell Mama?
PEGGY. I didn't think you'd want me to.
PAIGE. *(Into phone.)* Is Trey there? ... Paige Walker.
ROSEANNE. Somebody needs to tell her. I'd rather it not be Sherry. I can just imagine her next letter home: Greetings, your Mother-kins. Sweet Roseanne sent me some of her things today.

(LIGHTS come up in Aneece's bedroom. ANEECE emerges from the bathroom, holding her stomach. SHE sits carefully down on the bed and places the telephone next to her. SHE stares hard at the phone.)

ROSEANNE. I'll let you go, Peggy. I think I'll vacuum the attic.
PEGGY. Bye, Rose.

(THEY hang up. LIGHTS go out over ROSEANNE. PAIGE starts to pace. We hear a CLAP OF THUNDER which registers with PEGGY. SHE goes to the "window" and watches the RAIN. SHE seems lost in thought.)

PAIGE. (*Into phone.*) So that's what I'm known as around your dorm — "Paige the Panther?" ... Forget it. I said forget it, Trey. It's all over. You must have known I was eventually going to figure it out. I can think — ... NO, TREY! I CAN THINK OF A LOT OF OTHER THINGS I'D RATHER BE DOING THAN ENTERTAINING YOU AND YOUR HORNY DRINKING BUDDIES. You're a very attractive man, Trey Foster. Too bad you're not gay.

(*SHE hangs up with a flourish, grinning at the thought of what SHE has just accomplished. LIGHTS fade out. Another CLAP OF THUNDER. ANEECE dials her phone.*)

PEGGY. (*A sudden thought.*) The car windows are down.

(*SHE starts out of the room just as her phone RINGS. SHE goes to the phone.*)

PEGGY. Hello?
ANEECE. (*Still clutching her abdomen.*) I want to talk to my mother.
PEGGY. Is that *you,* Aneece?
ANEECE. Where's Mama?
PEGGY. She's here, but —
ANEECE. Put her on.
PEGGY. You know I can't.

ANEECE. (*Angrily.*) This is an ultimatum, Peggy. Are you listening? If I don't hear mama's voice on this telephone within the next two minutes, I'm cutting all ties. (*Silence.*) Goddamnit, Peggy. Did you hear what I said? It's over between Mama and me. (*Silence.*) PEGGY?

PEGGY. (*Helplessly.*) It's raining, Aneece.

ANEECE. I don't give a shit.

PEGGY. Mama won't even go into the bathroom when it's raining. She says the pipes invite lightning into our homes.

ANEECE. Where is she? Is she hiding in the closet? Is she sitting on the floor of her closet, dressed in that damn rubber suit she made us buy her ten years ago?

PEGGY. No, Aneece. She's in bed, reading. Like a normal person.

ANEECE. Then tell her to come to the phone. Like a normal person.

(*PEGGY doesn't reply.*)

ANEECE. I'm not tiptoeing around her phobias anymore.

PEGGY. Why now, Aneece? Why do you want to test her right *now?*

ANEECE. (*Hint of desperation.*) I *need* her.

PEGGY. (*Gently.*) Then come home. Come see her.

ANEECE. I have to talk to her tonight, Peggy. For Chrissakes, would you —

PEGGY. Let *me* help, Aneece.

ANEECE. (*Quickly.*) No.

PEGGY. I want to. I want to do some—

ANEECE. No.

PEGGY. You've never come to me, never asked me for anything.

ANEECE. What you can do for me right now is to put Mama on the phone. That's all I want from you. All I've ever wanted, Peggy — just let Mama and me come to our own terms.

PEGGY. She won't do it. I won't ask her because she won't do it.

ANEECE. (*Stunned.*) You won't even *ask* her?

PEGGY. She's not well right now.

ANEECE. I don't believe what I'm hearing!

PEGGY. Talk to *me*, Aneece. *Me*.

ANEECE. I don't want you, Peggy. I *don't like* you. (*She is crying now.*)

PEGGY. (*Desperately.*) What have *I* ever done?

ANEECE. No, Peggy.

PEGGY. (*Insistent.*) I want to know what it is I've done.

ANEECE. I can't handle that one right now.

PEGGY. (*Frightened.*) Handle *what?* You're not making any sense.

ANEECE. I just cannot —

PEGGY. (*Screaming.*) HANDLE WHAT?

ANEECE. You and Vincent.

PEGGY. (*Incredulously.*) Vincent?

ANEECE. You're doing the same thing to Mama you did to Vincent.

PEGGY. What in God's name are you talking about?

ANEECE. The way you strangled him.

PEGGY. (*Confused.*) Strang–

ANEECE. Clinging to him like some kind of parasite, sucking all the life out of him.

PEGGY. (*In tears.*) He was *dying*.

ANEECE. (*Overlapping.*) He couldn't breathe, Peggy.

PEGGY. (*Overlapping.*) I wanted to be close to him for as long as I–

ANEECE. (*Overlapping.*) He spent the last month of his life choking. He wanted to run.

PEGGY. Lies.

ANEECE. To run away, Peggy. He told me that. He wanted to run somewhere, anywhere you couldn't find him. Where his mind could be freed from thinking incessantly about the leukemia. With you that was impossible. Always the cloying, the hanging on, the constant reminder of the inevitable.

PEGGY. You're lying. You never talked to Vincent.

ANEECE. He called me, Peggy. Several times.

PEGGY. You're making all this up. I wish to God I knew why.

ANEECE. He had to have someone to talk to. Before those last two weeks at the hospice, there was no one.

PEGGY. He had *me*. Vincent and I — we fought it together.

ANEECE. No, Peggy. You showed him nothing but fear. With Vincent, with our beloved father, with anyone who posed the slightest threat to your neat, tidy little world, you just rolled over and played dead. No one in this family is any kind of a fighter and we can thank you and Mama for that. You both taught us cowardice so well.

PEGGY. (*Exploding.*) You go straight to hell!

ANEECE. Peggy — I'm already there.

(*Very long pause, then slowly ANEECE hangs up the phone. SHE lies back in bed and closes her eyes, one hand massaging her abdomen. PEGGY sobs softly, still holding the telephone handset in her hand. SHE takes a very long time to hang up the phone, then falls crumpled into her rocking chair. The LIGHTS dim around her. ANEECE opens her eyes, goes to her nightstand and fumbles for her cigarettes and lighter. SHE tries to light a cigarette; her hand is shaking and it takes a couple of attempts for her to succeed. SHE then retreats to her bed. SHE imagines a telephone conversation with her mother:*)

ANEECE. Hello? Is that you, Mama? Your
voice is quivering. You sound frightened. I'm
afraid too, Mama. Of different things. Of noises
in the middle of the night. Of being — You used to
call me the antisocial daughter. Remember?
"Why, here's the girls," you would announce to
your friends. "There's Roseanne with the sad
brown eyes, and Audrey so proud of her little
curtsy. And there hiding behind the sofa is
Aneece. She's anti-social, you see." Well, the
label stuck, Mama. I'm the loner, doing
everything my own way. When things click I
come home, pat myself on the back and share my
success with a bottle. And when my days *don't* go
so well, the bottle's still there to comfort me. (*A
beat.*) For a while at least. (*SHE takes a long drag
of the cigarette.*) I hate it all, Mama. You can't
possibly know what this feels like. But you *do*
know what it's like to be afraid. You've lived
through so many sleepless nights waiting for
Daddy to come home — listening for him to unlock
that back door. If it seemed like an eternity it
meant he was having trouble with the key and the
lock. And we all knew what *that* meant — Daddy
was too far gone for anything but blind drunken
rage. You used to pray out loud, Mama. I could
hear you. Roseanne would cover her ears and
Peggy would be locked in the bathroom with
Audrey, but I could hear every word. You'd pray to
God that for this one night Daddy would walk
right up to the door, put the key in the lock and

lumber in like a man who'd just had a few beers and was ready to sleep it off. I can still hear him at the back door, Mama. And I can still hear the prayers — "Our Father Who art in Heaven, don't let him kill us tonight." (*SHE takes another long drag, thinking.*) Now years later, alone in my apartment I can still hear him at the door. And I'm still afraid. (*Pause.*) I want to mend things with you, Mama. I want to wipe the slate clean. Maybe we can start talking each other through a few of these nights — scaring away the phantoms with the sound of our voices. (*THUNDER.*) I hear the thunder too, Mama. You better go. Call me again some time. I'd almost forgotten what your voice sounded like.

(*The LIGHTS in Aneece's bedroom dim. We hear the sound of a steady RAIN which continues under Peggy's phone monologue which follows. ANEECE lies down in bed and pulls the covers up around her. LIGHTS go out here. PEGGY gets up from the rocker and goes to the phone. SHE touches the receiver tentatively as if trying to find the courage to call someone. Finally, SHE picks up the handset, turns through her tel-address book and dials a number.*)

PEGGY. (*On phone.*) This is Peggy — Mrs. *Vincent* Reese. Is this Dr. Edwards? ... I'm very sorry to be disturbing you at home on a Sunday

night, doctor, but I'm — well, I have some
questions. I think there are some things Vincent
may have told you during his last days there at the
hospice. I know you two talked quite a bit — ...
Well, I thought it was time I faced a few things. I
think I'm ready now.

(*SHE takes the phone with her and goes to the
rocking chair. LIGHTS   fade to total
BLACKOUT. MUSIC plays for a moment,
then MONDAY MORNING. LIGHTS come up
in Audrey's den and Aneece's bedroom.
ANEECE sits on the bed, half-dressed for
work, the telephone in her lap, its receiver
held in the crook of her neck as SHE puts on
her shoes. The phone RINGS in Audrey's den.
AUDREY pads sleepily in on the third or
fourth ring. SHE wears a man's robe.*)

AUDREY. Hello?
ANEECE. Audrey?
AUDREY. Is that you, Aneece? What time is
it?
ANEECE. (*Looking at her watch.*) Must be
seven for you.
AUDREY. Is something wrong?
ANEECE. No. I wanted to apologize. For the
other night.
AUDREY. You don't have to.
ANEECE. I do have to. I know I said some
things that hurt you and I'm sorry.

AUDREY. It's all right, Aneece. Harry's home. Everything's okay now.

ANEECE. Does he know about Rothschild?

AUDREY. Yes. He cried. I've never seen Harry cry sober.

ANEECE. He must have really liked that little blockhead.

AUDREY. He didn't cry for Rothschild, Aneece. He cried for me. He said I'd lost something very special and he didn't think he'd be able to get it back. And then his voice got soft and whispery, and you know what he said to me, Aneece? He said I deserved another little boy and he wouldn't waste any time making this one. But instead of going out to his woodworking shop in the garage, he just turned and kissed me and then — I get chillbumps telling it, Aneece — he carried me back to the bedroom and he says with a smile, "Let's work on this one together."

ANEECE. Who'd have guessed Harry would turn into such a romantic?

AUDREY. So I'm all right now. In fact, I'm more than all right. And it's going to work out for you too, Aneece, because all of us, we've all paid our dues. It's time good things started happening for us.

ANEECE. (*Smiling.*) Is that what the little pamphlet says? The one you asked Amanda for?

AUDREY. No. It talks about cutting down on caffeine and getting more exercise.

ANEECE. (*Laughing.*) You're crazy.

AUDREY. It's in the genes.

(*The LIGHTS go down over both AUDREY and
ANEECE as LIGHTS come up in Roseanne's
kitchen and Dust's living space. ROSEANNE
stands at her counter, dialing her phone. The
phone in Dust's room RINGS several times.
No one enters to answer it. With each ring
ROSEANNE seems to sink deeper into gloom.
Then just as SHE starts to hang up, Dust's
answering machine clicks on.*)

DUST'S RECORDED VOICE. I'm not home
right now. If this is Mr. Moseley, the rent check is
in the mail. I swear it. If this is Venus, you can't
borrow any more ginseng tea. I'm all out. I'll be
out the next time you call, too. And if this is Peggy
– dear worrisome Peggy – I say unto thee: Worry
no more. William has escaped my clutches and is
now gobbling up the scenery along Pacific
Highway 101. At the sound of the beep, caller may
leave me a message or sing me a dirty love song.
Tata!

(*SOUND of BEEP. ROSEANNE doesn't seem to
know what to say. Finally SHE gives Dust's
machine a loud raspberry. SHE hangs up,
smiling smugly. LIGHTS fade out in both
places and come up in Peggy's empty sitting
room and Paige's empty dorm room. We hear
PAIGE'S VOICE just outside her room.*)

PAIGE. Goodbye, Leonard. Thank you for a beautiful evening. Watching the sun rise while you recite the periodic table of chemical elements is an experience I'll always hold dear. (*SHE enters and flops down on her bed. To herself:*) Feast or famine.

(*PEGGY walks into her sitting room. SHE carries a pad and pencil. SHE sits down at the desk, glances at the pad, and dials. The phone in Paige's room RINGS.*)

PAIGE. Hello?

PEGGY. Paige? It's Peggy.

PAIGE. Hi, Peggy.

PEGGY. Mama wanted me to call each of you.

PAIGE. What's wrong?

PEGGY. There was an accident.

PAIGE. You're not talking about the fish, are you?

PEGGY. No. The fish was Wednesday night.

PAIGE. Something happened since then?

PEGGY. Yes. Last night. At the bingo parlor. It was late. She insisted on going up there. She said it would calm her nerves. I let her go by herself. That was a mistake. (*A breath.*) It got to be real late and Mama hadn't gotten back yet. I thought she'd had a wreck or something. She said her eyes cross up on her when she drives at night. Finally I got a call from Mr. Biggers.

PAIGE. (*Interrupting.*) She said her eyes do
what at night?

PEGGY. What?

PAIGE. Her eyes – you said they – ?

PEGGY. Cross.

PAIGE. I've never heard her say that before.
I'll bet she's a sight when that happens. (*A beat,
then BOTH burst out laughing.*)

PEGGY. She's afraid they'll stick. She
actually said that.

PAIGE. No, Peggy.

PEGGY. She said they'd stick that way and
she'd never be able to see her friends again. I
wanted to say, "Sure you can still see your
friends, Mama. In fact, there'll be twice as many
of them." But I didn't say it. I bit my tongue.

PAIGE. Are you sick, Peggy?

PEGGY. I'm fine.

PAIGE. You're sure?

PEGGY. Of course I'm sure. Let me tell you
about the bingo parlor.

PAIGE. You said there was an accident.

PEGGY. Yes. Mr. Biggers said they were
taking Mama to the hospital. She'd been elbowed
in the forehead by this woman who had just won a
microwave. (*Again THEY laugh, PEGGY trying
hard to suppress it.*)

PAIGE. That's where she is now?

PEGGY. Until tomorrow at least. The doctor
said it was a concussion. He wants to keep her
under observation for a while.

PAIGE. (*Wiping her eyes.*) Mama's had the worse luck these last couple of years.

PEGGY. We've all been through some bad times.

PAIGE. But everybody just keeps hanging on. It's like that stupid thing Roseanne used to say — "When you get to the end of your rope, tie a knot and hang on."

PEGGY. How about Aneece's version — "When you get to the end of your rope, tie one on and hang it all." (*THEY both laugh.*)

PAIGE. But Sherry's — now, Sherry's takes the prize — "When you get to the end of your rope, metamorphosize into something with wings." (*THEY laugh harder.*)

PAIGE. We're overdue for a homecoming, Peggy.

PEGGY. Why don't you all try to make it for Christmas?

PAIGE. Or Thanksgiving. Remember how Audrey used to make the turkey sing and dance?

PEGGY. Don't remind me.

PAIGE. I'm really looking forward to seeing everyone again.

PEGGY. I know Mama misses her baby.

PAIGE. Peggy — would you call us a family?

PEGGY. (*Thinking.*) A family?

PAIGE. Would you say like by some special definition of the word, we're still a family?

PEGGY. I don't know why not. (*A beat.*) If our telephone bills count for anything.

PAIGE. Bye, Peggy. Give my love to Mama.
PEGGY. I will. Good-bye.

(*The LIGHTS in Paige's room go out. PEGGY hangs up the phone and drums her fingers on the desk for a moment, thinking. SHE looks at the pad, then at the phone. Finally, SHE pushes herself away from the desk. As if her mother were in the room:*)

PEGGY. I'll phone the others later, Mama. I haven't even had breakfast yet.

(*Stage goes BLACK as PEGGY starts out of the room. MUSIC comes up.*)

END OF PLAY

COSTUME PLOT

PEGGY

FRIDAY NIGHT: Plum skirt and blouse with cravate, shoes, stockings.

VERY EARLY SATURDAY MORNING: Nightgown and bathrobe, slippers.

LATER SATURDAY MORNING: Same.

LATE SATURDAY NIGHT: Beige vest sweater, blouse, gray skirt, shoes, stockings.

LATE SUNDAY MORNING: Same as LATER SATURDAY MORNING.

SUNDAY NIGHT: Cardigan sweater, blouse, skirt, shoes, stockings.

MONDAY MORNING: Same as LATER SATURDAY MORNING.

ANEECE

FRIDAY NIGHT: a) Bath towel
               b) Bathrobe
               c) Black formal dress,
               dress shoes, stockings.

VERY EARLY SATURDAY MORNING: Green surgical pants, white dress shirt.

LATER SATURDAY MORNING: Same

LATE SATURDAY NIGHT: Same

SUNDAY NIGHT: Same with gray pullover sweater and socks.

MONDAY MORNING: Dress suit, dress shoes and stockings.

ROSEANNE:

FRIDAY NIGHT: Jeans, blouse, sneakers, apron, bandana.
VERY EARLY SATURDAY MORNING: Same
LATE SATURDAY NIGHT: Same.
LATE SUNDAY MORNING: Navy blue suit, skirt, dress shoes, stockings.
SUNDAY NIGHT: Same with apron.
MONDAY MORNING: Nightgown and bathrobe, slippers.

AUDREY:

FRIDAY NIGHT: Black strapless gown with bright red heart on chest, dress shoes.
VERY EARLY SATURDAY MORNING: Same.
LATER SATURDAY MORNING: Pink sweater, jeans, sneakers.
LATE SATURDAY NIGHT: Same.
SUNDAY NIGHT: Red flannel shirt, jeans, sneakers.
MONDAY MORNING: Man's robe, slippers.

DUST:

FRIDAY NIGHT: Leotards with oversized pullover shirt.

VERY EARLY SATURDAY MORNING: Same.

LATER SATURDAY MORNING: Leotards with pullover sweater.

LATE SUNDAY MORNING: White poncho, leotards, shoes.

SUNDAY NIGHT: Same.

PAIGE:

FRIDAY NIGHT: Cowboy boots, shorts, man's shirt.

VERY EARLY SATURDAY MORNING: University of Texas jersey.

LATER SATURDAY MORNING: Jersey with jeans, sneakers and socks.

LATE SATURDAY NIGHT: Same, then magenta dress, belted, dress shoes.

LATE SUNDAY MORNING: T-shirt, jeans, sneakers.

SUNDAY NIGHT: Same.

MONDAY MORNING: Same with windbreaker.

PROPERTY PLOT

PEGGY:

PRESET ON WRITING TABLE: notebook,
file folder, insurance forms, tel-adress book.

PRESET ON BOOKCASE: hardcover books

PRESET IN WRITING TABLE DRAWER:
additional pads and pencils.

PERSONAL PROPS: pad and pencil, cup of
coffee, photo album, knitting needles and yarn,
dishcloth, *Memphis Commercial Appeal Mid
South Magazine* (Sunday magazine).

ANEECE:

PRESET ON TABLE: tel-address book,
briefcase with paperwork and *Wall Street
Journal*, vodka bottle, glass, cigarettes.

ROSEANNE:

PRESET ON COUNTER: broken blender,
screwdriver, salt and pepper shakers, bottle of
ketchup, bottle of steak sauce, sugar bowl, glass,
dish towel, coffee cup.

PRESET UNDER COUNTER: paper towels,
bottle of Scotch.

AUDREY:

PRESET ON CABINET: trophies, photograph of Harry.

PRESET ON CHILD'S CHAIR: Rothschild.

PRESET ON PHONE TABLE: Yellow Pages, *Redbook Magazine*.

PRESET BELOW PHONE TABLE: glass of water.

PERSONAL PROPS: pad and pencil.

DUST:

PRESET ON FLOOR: scraps of paper, tape recorder, throw pillows, candles, bowl of raisins.

PERSONAL PROPS: daypack with clothes.

PAIGE:

PRESET IN MILK CRATES ON FLOOR: beer bottles, text books, romance novels.

PERSONAL PROP: piece of paper with Trey's phone number.

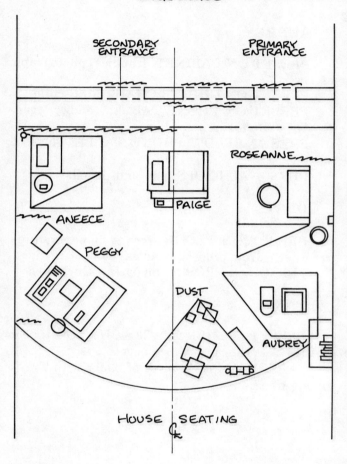

BACK STAGE

SECONDARY ENTRANCE

PRIMARY ENTRANCE

ANEECE

PAIGE

ROSEANNE

PEGGY

DUST

AUDREY

HOUSE SEATING

SCENE DESIGN
"BELLES"

Other Publications for Your Interest

TALKING WITH...

(LITTLE THEATRE)

By JANE MARTIN

11 women—Bare stage

Here, at last, is the collection of eleven extraordinary monologues for eleven actresses which had them on their feet cheering at the famed Actors Theatre of Louisville—audiences, critics and, yes, even jaded theatre professionals. The mysteriously pseudonymous Jane Martin is truly a "find", a new writer with a wonderfully idiosyncratic style, whose characters alternately amuse, move and frighten us always, however, speaking to us from the depths of their souls. The characters include a baton twirler who has found God through twirling; a fundamentalist snake handler, an ex-rodeo rider crowded out of the life she has cherished by men in 3-piece suits who want her to dress up "like Minnie damn Mouse in a tutu"; an actress willing to go to any length to get a job; and an old woman who claims she once saw a man with "cerebral walrus" walk into a McDonald's and be healed by a Big Mac. "Eleven female monologues, of which half a dozen verge on brilliance."—London Guardian. "Whoever (Jane Martin) is, she's a writer with an original imagination."—Village Voice. "With Jane Martin, the monologue has taken on a new poetic form, intensive in its method and revelatory in its impact."—Philadelphia Inquirer. "A dramatist with an original voice . . . (these are) tales about enthusiasms that become obsessions, eccentric confessionals that levitate with religious symbolism and gladsome humor."—N.Y. Times. *Talking With . . .* is the 1982 winner of the American Theatre Critics Association Award for Best Regional Play. (#22009)

(Royalty, $60-$40.
If individual monologues are done separately: Royalty, $15-$10.)

HAROLD AND MAUDE

(ADVANCED GROUPS—COMEDY)

By COLIN HIGGINS

9 men, 8 women—Various settings

Yes: *the Harold and Maude!* This is a stage adaptation of the wonderful movie about the suicidal 19 year-old boy who finally learns how to truly *live* when he meets up with that delightfully whacky octogenarian, Maude. Harold is the proverbial Poor Little Rich Kid. His alienation has caused him to attempt suicide several times, though these attempts are more cries for attention than actual attempts. His peculiar attachment to Maude, whom he meets at a funeral (a mutual passion), is what saves him—and what captivates us. This new stage version, a hit in France directed by the internationally-renowned Jean-Louis Barrault, will certainly delight both afficionados of the film and new-comers to the story. "Offbeat upbeat comedy."—Christian Science Monitor. (#10032)

(Royalty, $60-$40.)

Other Publications for Your Interest

AGNES OF GOD
(LITTLE THEATRE—DRAMA)

By JOHN PIELMEIER

3 women—1 set (bare stage)

Doctor Martha Livingstone, a court-appointed psychiatrist, is asked to determine the sanity of a young nun accused of murdering her own baby. Mother Miriam Ruth, the nun's superior, seems bent on protecting Sister Agnes from the doctor, and Livingstone's suspicions are immediately aroused. In searching for solutions to various mysteries (who killed the baby? Who fathered the child?) Livingstone forces all three women, herself included, to face some harsh realities in their own lives, and to re-examine the meaning of faith and the commitment of love. "Riveting, powerful, electrifying new drama . . . three of the most magnificent performances you will see this year on any stage anywhere . . . the dialogue crackles."—Rex Reed, N.Y. Daily News. ". . . outstanding play . . . deals intelligently with questions of religion and psychology."—Mel Gussow, N.Y. Times. ". . . unquestionably blindingly theatrical . . . cleverly executed blood and guts evening in the theatre . . . three sensationally powered performances calculated to wring your withers."—Clive Barnes, N.Y. Post.   (#236)

Royalty, $60-$40
(Posters available)

COME BACK TO THE
5 & DIME,
JIMMY DEAN, JIMMY DEAN
(ADVANCED GROUPS—DRAMA)

By ED GRACZYK

1 man, 8 women—Interior

In a small-town dime store in West Texas, the Disciples of James Dean gather for their twentieth reunion. Now a gaggle of middle-aged women, the Disciples were teenagers when Dean filmed "Giant" two decades ago in nearby Marfa. One of them, an extra in the film, has a child whom she says was conceived by Dean on the "Giant" set; the child is the Jimmy Dean of the title. The ladies' reminiscences mingle with flash-backs to their youth; then the arrival of a stunning and momentarily unrecognized woman sets off a series of confrontations that upset their self-deceptions and expose their well-hidden disappointments. "Full of homespun humor . . . surefire comic gems."—N.Y. Post. "Captures convincingly the atmosphere of the 1950s."—Women's Wear Daily.   (#5147)

(Royalty, $60-$40.)

Other Publications for Your Interest

A WEEKEND NEAR MADISON

(LITTLE THEATRE—COMIC DRAMA)

By KATHLEEN TOLAN

2 men, 3 women—Interior

This recent hit from the famed Actors Theatre of Louisville, a terrific ensemble play about male-female relationships in the 80's, was praised by *Newsweek* as "warm, vital, glowing . . . full of wise ironies and unsentimental hopes". The story concerns a weekend reunion of old college friends now in their early thirties. The occasion is the visit of Vanessa, the queen bee of the group, who is now the leader of a lesbian/feminist rock band. Vanessa arrives at the home of an old friend who is now a psychiatrist hand in hand with her naif-like lover, who also plays in the band. Also on hand are the psychiatrist's wife, a novelist suffering from writer's block; and his brother, who was once Vanessa's lover and who still loves her. In the course of the weekend, Vanessa reveals that she and her lover desperately want to have a child—and she tries to persuade her former male lover to father it, not understanding that he might have some feelings about the whole thing. *Time Magazine* heard "the unmistakable cry of an infant hit . . . Playwright Tolan's work radiates promise and achievement." (#25051)

(Royalty, $60-$40.)

PASTORALE

(LITTLE THEATRE—COMEDY)

By DEBORAH EISENBERG

3 men, 4 women—Interior
(plus 1 or 2 bit parts and 3 optional extras)

"Deborah Eisenberg is one of the freshest and funniest voices in some seasons."—Newsweek. Somewhere out in the country Melanie has rented a house and in the living room she, her friend Rachel who came for a weekend but forgets to leave, and their school friend Steve (all in their mid-20s) spend nearly a year meandering through a mental landscape including such concerns as phobias, friendship, work, sex, slovenliness and epistemology. Other people happen by: Steve's young girlfriend Celia, the virtuous and annoying Edie, a man who Melanie has picked up in a bar, and a couple who appear during an intense conversation and observe the sofa is on fire. The lives of the three friends inevitably proceed and eventually draw them, the better prepared perhaps by their months on the sofa, in separate directions. "The most original, funniest new comic voice to be heard in New York theater since Beth Henley's 'Crimes of the Heart.'"—N.Y. Times. "A very funny, stylish comedy."—The New Yorker. "Wacky charm and wayward wit."—New York Magazine. "Delightful."—N.Y. Post. "Uproarious . . . the play is a world unto itself, and it spins."—N.Y. Sunday Times. (#18016)

(Royalty, $50-$35.)

Other Publications for Your Interest

THE OCTETTE BRIDGE CLUB
(LITTLE THEATRE—COMIC DRAMA)

By P.J. BARRY

1 man, 8 women—Interior

There are no less than *eight wonderful roles for women* in this delightful sentimental comedy about American life in the 30's and 40's. On alternate Friday evenings, eight sisters meet to play bridge, gossip and generally entertain themselves. They are a group portrait right out of Norman Rockwell America. The first act takes place in 1934; the second act, ten years later, during a Hallowe'en costume/bridge party. Each sister acts out her character, climaxing with the youngest sister's hilarious belly dance as Salome. She, whom we have perceived in the first act as being somewhat emotionally distraught, has just gotten out of a sanitarium, and has realized that she must cut the bonds that have tied her to her smothering family and strike out on her own. This wonderful look at an American family in an era far more innocent and naive than our own was quite a standout at the Actors Theatre of Louisville Humana Festival of New American Plays. The play did not succeed with Broadway's jaded critics (which these days just may be a mark in its favor); but we truly believe it is a perfect play for Everybody Else; particularly, community theatres with hordes of good actresses clamoring for roles. "One of the most charming plays to come to the stage this season . . . a delightful, funny, moving glimpse of the sort of lives we are all familiar with—our own."—NY Daily News "Counterpunch".   (#17056)

(Royalty, $60-$40.)

BIG MAGGIE
(LITTLE THEATRE—DRAMA)

By JOHN B. KEANE

5 men, 6 women—Exterior/Interior

We are very proud to be making available for U.S. production the most popular play by one of contemporary Ireland's most beloved playwrights. The title character is the domineering mother of four wayward, grown-up children, each determined to go his own way, as Youth will do—and each likely headed in the wrong direction. Maggie has been burdened with a bibulous, womanizing husband. Now that he has died, though, she is free to exercise some control over the lives of herself and her family, much to the consternation of her children. Wonderful character parts abound in this tightly-constructed audience-pleaser, none finer than the role of Maggie—a gem of a part for a middle-aged actress! "The feminist awareness that informs the play gives it an intriguing texture, as we watch it unfold against a colorfully detailed background of contemporary rural Ireland. It is at times like hearing Ibsen with an Irish brogue."—WWD.   (#4637)

(Royalty, $50-$40.)

Other Publications for Your Interest

THE CURATE SHAKESPEARE AS YOU LIKE IT

(LITTLE THEATRE—COMEDY)

By DON NIGRO

4 men, 3 women—Bare stage

This extremely unusual and original piece is subtitled: ''The record of one company's attempt to perform the play by William Shakespeare''. When the very prolific Mr. Nigro was asked by a professional theatre company to adapt *As You Like It* so that it could be performed by a company of seven he, of course, came up with a completely original play about a rag-tag group of players comprised of only seven actors led by a dotty old curate who nonetheless must present Shakespeare's play; and the dramatic interest, as well as the comedy, is in their hilarious attempts to impersonate all of Shakespeare's multitude of characters. The play has had numerous productions nationwide, all of which have come about through word of mouth. We are very pleased to make this ''underground comic classic'' widely available to theatre groups who like their comedy wide open and theatrical. (#5742)

(Royalty, $50-$25.)

SEASCAPE WITH SHARKS AND DANCER

(LITTLE THEATRE—DRAMA)

By DON NIGRO

1 man, 1 woman—Interior

This is a fine new play by an author of great talent and promise. We are very glad to be introducing Mr. Nigro's work to a wide audience with *Seascape With Sharks and Dancer*, which comes directly from a sold-out, critically acclaimed production at the world-famous Oregon Shakespeare Festival. The play is set in a beach bungalow. The young man who lives there has pulled a lost young woman from the ocean. Soon, she finds herself trapped in his life and torn between her need to come to rest somewhere and her certainty that all human relationships turn eventually into nightmares. The struggle between his tolerant and gently ironic approach to life and her strategy of suspicion and attack becomes a kind of war about love and creation which neither can afford to lose. In other words, this is quite an offbeat, wonderful love story We would like to point out that the play also contains a wealth of excellent *monologue* and *scene material.* (#21060)

(Royalty, $50-$35.)

Other Publications for Your Interest

I'M NOT RAPPAPORT
(LITTLE THEATRE—COMEDY)
By HERB GARDNER

5 men, 2 women—Exterior

Just when we thought there would never be another joyous, laugh-filled evening on Broadway, along came this delightful play to restore our faith in the Great White Way. If you thought *A Thousand Clowns* was wonderful, wait til you take a look at *I'm Not Rappaport!* Set in a secluded spot in New York's Central Park, the play is about two octogenarians determined to fight off all attempts to put them out to pasture. Talk about an odd couple! Nat is a lifelong radical determined to fight injustice (real or imagined) who is also something of a spinner of fantasies. He has a delightful repertoire of eccentric personas, which makes the role an actor's dream. The other half of this unlikely partnership is Midge, a Black apartment super who spends his days in the park hiding out from tenants, who want him to retire. "Rambunctiously funny."—N.Y. Post. "A warm and entertaining evening."—W.W. Daily. **Tony Award Winner, Best Play 1986. Posters.**

(#11071)

(Royalty, $60-$40.)

CROSSING DELANCEY
(LITTLE THEATRE—COMEDY)
By SUSAN SANDLER

2 men, 3 women—Comb. Interior/Exterior.

Isabel is a young Jewish woman who lives alone and works in a NYC bookshop. When she is not pining after a handsome author who is one of her best customers, she is visiting her grandmother—who lives by herself in the "old neighborhood", Manhattan's Lower East Side. Isabel is in no hurry to get married, which worries her grandmother. The delightfully nosey old lady hires an old friend who is—can you believe this in the 1980's?—a matchmaker. Bubbie and the matchmaker come up with a Good Catch for their Isabel—Sam, a young pickle vendor. Same is no *schlemiel,* though. He likes Isabel; but he knows he is going to have to woo her, which he proceeds to do. When Isabel realizes what a cad the author is, and what a really nice man Sam is, she begins to respond; and the end of the play is really a beginning, ripe with possibilities for Isabel and "An amusing interlude for theatregoers who may have thought that simple romance and sentimentality had long since been relegated to television sitcoms...tells its unpretentious story believeably, rarely trying to make its gag lines, of which there are many, upstage its narration or outshine its heart."—N.Y. Times. "A warm and loving drama...a welcome addition to the growing body of Jewish dramatic work in this country."—Jewish Post and Opinion.

(#5739)

(Royalty, $50-$40.)